BECOME TH...
LOVER NATU...
TO BE!

Using Dr. Barbara DeBetz's clear, step-by-step instructions, you will reach a state of clarified awareness that allows you to relax, shed sexual hangups, and even explore your wildest sexual fantasies.

Fascinating quizzes, easy-to-do exercises, and revealing case studies explain techniques that will liberate your full sensuality and open the door to a new world of erotic delights. Perfected by use in a highly respected sex therapy program, *Erotic Focus* brings satisfying results that will help you and your partner discover a more fulfilling and joyful sexual intimacy.

EROTIC FOCUS

"Straightforward, easy to read and quite original ... the technique will be of interest to patients and therapists alike."

—Patricia Raley, author of
*Making Love: How to Be Your Own
Sex Therapist*

BARBARA DEBETZ, M.D., is on the faculty of psychiatry at Columbia University with a private practice in New York City. She is the author of a professional textbook, and her articles have appeared in *Vogue, Self, Mademoiselle,* and *Cosmopolitan.*

SAMM SINCLAIR BAKER has been called "America's Leading Self-Help Author" by *The New York Times.* He is co-author of *The Complete Scarsdale Medical Diet* (with Dr. Tarnower), and *The Doctor's Quick Weight Loss Diet* (with Dr. Stillman).

EROTIC FOCUS
THE NEW WAY TO ENHANCE YOUR SEXUAL PLEASURE

Barbara DeBetz, M.D.
Diplomate, American Board of
Psychiatry & Neurology
and
Samm Sinclair Baker

A SIGNET BOOK

NEW AMERICAN LIBRARY

Illustrations by Randi Wasserman

SIGNET, SIGNET CLASSIC, MENTOR, ONYX, PLUME, MERIDIAN
AND NAL BOOKS are published by NAL PENGUIN INC.,
1633 Broadway, New York, New York 10019.

First Signet Printing, August, 1986

2 3 4 5 6 7 8 9 10

I dedicate this book in gratitude to:

All my patients, without whom this book would not exist;

All my colleagues who shared their knowledge and expertise so generously;

And to my mother, Herta Holstein, who always encouraged me to do what I wanted to do.

—Barbara DeBetz

To Natalie, without whose love and help nothing would be as possible and as rewarding.

—Samm Sinclair Baker

CONTENTS

EROTIC FOCUS
THE NEW WAY TO ENHANCE YOUR SEXUAL PLEASURE

INTRODUCTION: THE EROTIC FOCUS METHOD

We all want sexual pleasure at its peak, a total sexual fulfillment that combines ecstasy, communication, understanding and love. That's "supersex."

It's all yours through Erotic Focus—a simple technique proved by the results I've achieved with a great many women and men in my years of medical practice. With the help of my Erotic Focus ("E.F.") technique, you can enjoy not only greater sexual pleasure but also clearer thinking and more rewarding experiences and relationships.

You can learn the Erotic Focus method in minutes. The simple instructions are all in these pages. Every word will bring you closer to more sexual pleasure and fulfillment than you've ever experienced before. My emphasis in this book is on what you can *do* specifically for self-improvement, not on empty theory or abstract discussion.

Don't have any doubts about this: *My Erotic Focus technique can work for you if you will work with it.* This has been proven repeatedly in my experience with others in many different walks of life. You don't require any exceptional talents or abilities. Just follow the simple step-by-step guidelines faithfully and you'll get immediate rewards.

Through the use of E.F. you'll learn how to relieve an inhibiting overload of confusion and self-doubt that you may not know exists within you. You'll feel liberated because you'll have gained a clear understanding, leading to positive actions, greater intimacy, communication, respect, depth of emotion. The essential combination—seeing clearly and understanding fully—provides the most rewarding love and passion between caring individuals. The result is more successful, more fulfilling sex and love.

Using the technique is fun, too, as you get the benefits you want. The proof for you is in the reading and *doing*. I urge you to get started now. You have nothing to lose but possibly existing inhibitions and *mis*information which have limited your maximum enjoyment of sex and life up to now.

The state of Erotic Focus is one of *clarified awareness*, fully controlled by you. It enables you to "see" *into* and *through* a problem more readily, to find wanted directions and solutions. The result might be compared to cleaning a clouded, grimy window crystal clear so you can see through in precise, revealing detail.

By clearing away mental clutter, the exercise screens out extraneous, negative, detrimental concerns. E.F. acts to remove anxiety and stress which interfere with top sexual performance and enjoyment. Studies confirm that mental confusion, anxiety and turmoil are prime hindrances to fullest sexual functioning and pleasure for the normal individual.

Instead of being sidetracked or blocked by outside perplexities, or by lack of awareness or insights, the mind in Erotic Focus "shifts gears" and concentrates on the immediate involvement. The effect is that you attain a new dimension of greater participation and pleasure. Those using the method correctly report thrilling improvement and gratification due to their liberated sexual attitudes, release from tensions, and enhanced abilities.

The technique also promotes helpful, maximum muscle easing and subsequent control, at the same time as it alerts your mental facilities. This differs most desirably from nondirective meditation processes or other muscle relaxation procedures. While attaining a liberated mind in E.F., *your body too will actually be eased,* a proficient coordination between mind and body. This dual result is extremely beneficial since, otherwise, muscles usually tense up and, at the same time, function is slowed or impaired when the mind is occupied with worries, anxiety, unpleasant thoughts.

Through the Erotic Focus process you profit from a revitalizing concentration and boost of your *natural abilities,* often unrealized before. At once you progress rapidly to achieve the end result you want: *supersex.*

In addition to teaching you the Erotic Focus technique, so that you'll be able to use and apply it as you wish, I also provide easy-to-follow instructions on how to use E.F., plus specific expanded techniques, to help overcome common sexual dysfunctions. In men, widespread problems include pervading or occasional impotence, and/or premature ejaculation, and other dysfunctions. In women, the inability to achieve orgasms all or most of the time is quite prevalent, along with other difficulties. The clear, detailed explanations and step-by-step instructions for corrective treatments for these dysfunctions (which may affect almost anyone at some time or other) are enlightening, whether or not you need them right now. The information expands your understanding of sexual functioning and can be most valuable and useful if you or someone you are concerned about ever needs such help.

Sexual discovery about yourself by yourself is an unequaled joy. Erotic Focus will provide a new dimension of sexual pleasure for you and those close to you.

Note: You'll find many helpful case histories from my practice in this book. Names have been changed to conceal identities, and some cases are composites.

1 SEX INFORMATION QUIZ: DISCOVER YOUR SEXUAL QUOTIENT

In order for you to use the Erotic Focus method most effectively, it's helpful first to check your sexual knowledge. In my practice I always take a sexual history, regardless of the problem presented—whether sexual or not. I do this because sexuality is an integral element in the personality and well-being of each of us. As a psychiatrist it is vital that I explore all aspects of an individual's life, including sexual attitudes and habits. I have found that most persons, even those who don't complain about any sexual problems in particular, *can improve some aspect of their sexual lives*. That most probably applies to you also.

In your instance, since we are not face-to-face, I've devised an interesting and revealing self-test by which you can measure your current sexual knowledge. Taking the test is as easy as this:

You simply circle with a pencil either T (True) or F (False) after reading and considering each of the questions in the following listing. Then you compare your choices with my true-or-false answers. Thus you learn your individual rating. Whatever that score may turn out to be now, your Sexual Quotient will undoubtedly be higher by the time you finish this book.

One of the advantages of this self-quiz is that you can try to answer the questions honestly. You're not trying to impress anyone else, not a therapist, not a friend. Often when we're questioned by someone else or in an open group, there's always the possibility—consciously or not—that we give the answers that we feel would gain the most approval or get the highest marks.

The knowledge you gain from noting the correct answers to this self-quiz can lead you to functioning better and enjoying sex more. Much misinformation that may have misled you in the past will be cleared away. Your improved understanding can reveal mistakes you may have been making. You can avoid such errors and build on what you've learned—from now on. Answering the self-quiz, then noting where you were right or wrong, is a basic first step to the better sex you seek.

Sexual Quotient Self-Quiz: Rating Your Own S.Q.

Simply answer the twenty-five questions here by circling T (True) or F (False) to the best of your current knowledge. After you complete the quiz, compare your answer to each question with the correct answers which follow. You'll learn your S.Q. rating when you check your answers with the scoring system at the end of the quiz.

	TRUE	FALSE

1. Most women require stimulation of the clitoris (the small erectile organ near the entrance to the vagina), in addition to any other actions or manipulations, to achieve orgasm because the clitoris is the seat of female sexual pleasure   T   F

2. Stimulation of the clitoris is irritating to most women if done when they are not fully aroused sexually   T   F

3. Only mutual orgasms (both partners coming simultaneously) provide full sexual fulfillment   T   F

4. In a good sexual relationship, both partners always have ecstatic orgasms   T   F

5. About 10 percent of sexually active females do not and cannot ever attain orgasm   T   F

6. Only about 30 percent of women normally reach orgasm during intercourse with vaginal stimulation only   T   F

7. While a few alcoholic drinks may increase sexual responsiveness, too many lead to impotence in men . . . and lubrication difficulties in women   T   F

8. By nature as well as custom, the female is the passive partner . . . while the male is the aggressive one   T   F

9. Women normally take a longer time to become physically aroused than men   T   F

10. A woman's sexual desire and responsiveness naturally decrease after menopause   T   F

11. The length of a man's penis is directly correlated to the amount of sexual enjoyment of the female partner   T   F

12. Occasional difficulties by a man in attaining penis erection are indications of oncoming and eventually enduring impotence   T   F

13. Sexual arousal for men is related more

to *visual* stimulation . . . while women are more aroused by *touch*   T   F

14. Most sexually transmitted diseases—syphilis, gonorrhea, herpes, AIDS—are all treatable and curable now   T   F

15. For a woman to engage in intercourse or any other form of sexual activity while menstruating is medically harmful   T   F

16. The "rhythm method" as a means of contraception is not reliable because a woman may ovulate (shed eggs from her ovary) at irregular times   T   F

17. By the time a man reaches his fifties, his refractory periods (intervals between follow-up orgasms) can last up to twenty-four hours   T   F

18. Early morning erections in a man with erectile dysfunction (impotence) indicate a psychological rather than a physical cause for his dysfunction   T   F

19. The male testes (testicles) have a limited capacity to produce the supply of sperm   T   F

20. When the penis is fully erect, it is almost impossible for the male to urinate   T   F

21. Anxiety or tension can interrupt and prevent the normal sexual reflex of erection in men, and of orgasm in both women and men   T   F

22. People with sexual problems are almost always mentally disturbed   T   F

23. Most cases of premature ejaculation are due to anxiety rather than to a physical cause   T   F

24. Homosexual activities during adolescence clearly indicate the probability of lifetime homosexual preference (male or female)   T   F

25. Masturbation is an uncommon, unhealthy, perverted expression of sexuality in adolescents and adults of both sexes   T   F

ANSWERS TO SEX-QUIZ QUESTIONS

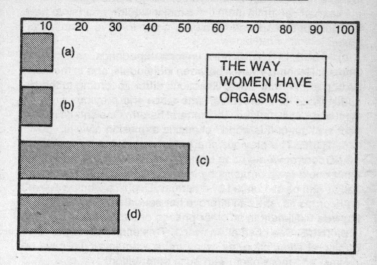

THE WAY
WOMEN HAVE
ORGASMS. . .

1. TRUE. The chart shows how women have orgasms:

(a) No orgasm at all—about 10 percent.

(b) No orgasm with partner . . . but through masturbation, including clitoris stimulation—about 10 percent.

(c) Orgasm during sexual intercourse, with direct or indirect clitoral stimulation—about 50 percent.

(d) Orgasm during sexual intercourse, no clitoral stimulation—about 30 percent.

2. TRUE. The primary erotic areas are the nipples, vaginal entrance and the clitoris. The most responsive area is the clitoris. However, many women do *not* enjoy clitoral stimulation unless they are fully aroused and lubricated; it can be irritating, sore, and a turn-off.

3. FALSE. The joint experience of two partners climaxing at the same time is for most a wonderful experience, but should never be considered essential for successful sexual intercourse. Being preoccupied with mutual orgasms usually interferes with a free-floating sense of sexual enjoyment. If it happens, fine. If not, each orgasm can be enjoyed separately. When a man (usually in later years) has just one orgasm, while the woman can have more orgasms, it wouldn't be fair to have her hold back and wait for him in order to have a mutual orgasm.

4. FALSE. Orgasm is not a uniform experience, especially in women. Response varies between individuals, and in the same person at different times. Reactions differ according to the circumstances of intercourse, time since the previous orgasm, level of arousal, fatigue, and general health. One should not expect an "out-of-this-world" climactic explosion always.

5. TRUE. The previous chart affirms this, but though about 10 percent of women don't climax, many who think that they can't could have orgasms by learning how to stimulate themselves and be stimulated by a partner. Even if a woman doesn't have orgasms, she can improve her sexual enjoyment by finding true fulfillment in all other phases of intercourse.

6. TRUE. See chart at Answer 1. This emphasizes the value of clitoral stimulation, as many more women would have orgasms, and more often, with such stimulation.

7. TRUE. A couple of drinks for social enjoyment can have a relaxing effect. But alcohol consumed in large quantities, or chronically, can cause sexual difficulties. As Shakespeare wrote, too much alcohol "provokes the desire, but it takes away the performance."

8. FALSE. By nature all human beings have sexual impulses. In the past it wasn't considered "ladylike" for a woman to show her sexual desires. In the last fifteen to twenty years, women have become progressively more "aggressive" sexually, knowing and telling their partners what they want. In a good sexual relationship, both partners may alternate between passive and aggressive sexual behavior.

9. TRUE. This difference is especially pronounced in the very young, as young males are stirred often just by looking at a girl while she has greater need for gentle caressing and stimulation of genital and nongenital areas. At all ages females usually require a longer time to be fully aroused.

10. FALSE AND TRUE. It's *true* that certain physiological changes take place in the female after menopause, which may or may not affect responsiveness. But the statement is basically *false* since menopause does *not* interfere psychologically with sexual desire, response, and enjoyment. A great many women experience *increased sexual desire* after menopause. There's no more fear of pregnancy, children are grown, leaving more time for the couple, and there are other similar-favorable factors.

11. FALSE. The size of the penis means little in sexual pleasure. Actually, if the penis is extremely large or wide, it can cause discomfort for the woman. The quality of mutual sharing and caring, the touching and caressing make intercourse most enjoyable and fulfilling, not the size of the equipment.

12. FALSE. Temporary erection problems can happen to almost every man at one time or another. The most common cause is *anxiety* which can drain the penis instantaneously of its blood supply, leading to a flaccid (limp) penis. Other causes include too much alcohol, and drugs that have a central nervous system depressant effect. If the erection difficulty occurs often, medical help is advisable to rule out any physical causes. (See Chapter 11.)

13. TRUE. It's well established that men can get sexually aroused readily by *visual* stimulation—seeing an appealing female, photos, visual fantasies. For women, *touch* is a leading factor, along with *emotional* reactions. These differences may be primarily cultural rather then physiological; with changing sex activity and attitudes now, arousal effects may change.

14. FALSE. Syphilis and gonorrhea are caused by specific microorganisms and, if treated properly by a physician, these dangerous diseases can be cured. Herpes is a viral infection, and no curative treatments have been found to this date. AIDS (Acquired Immune Deficiency Syndrome), occurring predominantly among homosexuals, presently remains very much an enigma regarding its course as well as treatment.

15. FALSE. There is no medical reason why a woman should refrain from intercourse or other sexual activity while menstruating. Old taboos about being "unclean," and concern over the sight and effects of menstrual blood, cause many to avoid intercourse. Some women report increased sex drive when menstruating, and enjoy sex very much during the period.

16. TRUE. This method is based on the concept that a woman is fertile only during the forty-eight hours after the ovum (female reproductive cell) travels from the ovary to the uterus and stays there until it dies if not fertilized. The rhythm method works for some couples, but isn't reliable because some women ovulate irregularly, and even those who ovulate regularly may ovulate spontaneously at any time under certain conditions. Some women even ovulate while menstruating.

17. TRUE. The period between orgasms for men is shortest in late teens through twenties. Then men may even be *multiorgasmic,* may climax several times in a row, and have many orgasms per day. This diminishes; as a man reaches the fifties, he usually has just one orgasm at a time, with the next generally as much as twelve to twenty-four hours later (there are exceptions). He can, of course, enjoy other sexual activities such as fondling, caressing, oral sex.

18. TRUE. This is one sign of "psychogenic" impotence—a psychological rather than physical reason for a man not getting erections. If psychological, he still has erections during sleep, not under his conscious control, and often an erection on awakening. If the problem is physical, there are usually fewer or no such erections. This can be determined in a sleep laboratory, with special monitoring equipment, and by visual observation (possible also by the partner at home). A physician should be consulted.

Here is what one of my patients, who suffered from psychological impotence, did. He wasn't convinced that he had erections during sleep, until he tried this ingenious test: He fastened a light paper strip (like a cigar band) snugly around his limp penis at bedtime. When he awakened in the morning, he saw that the paper band had split apart and *knew* he was physically able to have erections. His impotence disappeared with the treatment detailed in Chapter 11.

19. FALSE. The testicles continue to function in men indefinitely, though there may be a gradual decline in the rate of testosterone (male hormone) and sperm production. However, men even in their eighties and nineties have fathered children.

20. TRUE. The penis has two *separate* functions: urination and reproduction. During ejaculation, a small valve automatically closes the opening between the urethra canal and bladder so effectively that it is impossible in the healthy male for urine to escape through the penis during *ejaculation.* This also makes it difficult to urinate while a man has a full erection.

21. TRUE. When a person is anxious, the normal sexual responses and reflexes are interfered with in both sexes. In the tense male blood flows to his chest, arms, legs, other areas, preparing for an "emergency" or "survival" situation, rather than to engage in lovemaking. This impedes blood flow to the penis, inhibiting erection. The anxious female is afflicted similarly—she can't relax so her pelvic muscles would engage in the usual sequence leading to orgasm. Anxiety and tension are to some degree probably responsible for most sexual problems.

22. FALSE. Almost everyone has some sexual problem or difficulty at some time in life, not related to mental illness. The mentally ill person can also have sexual problems, but one is not necessarily related to the other.

23. TRUE. Premature ejaculation may occur to a man worried about his sexual performance, or due to anxiety about control over his orgasm. It's common in a young man starting his sexual life, but he usually learns quickly to control it. If the problem persists, it may require treatment—usually with a very favorable outcome.

24. FALSE. Most heterosexual people have had some homosexual experiences, especially when young—which they find enjoyable or frightening or both. It doesn't mean that the person is or will be homosexual. Many heterosexuals even enjoy homosexual fantasies occasionally during intercourse.

25. FALSE. Masturbation used to be thought sinful and harmful, but today it is considered normal for males and females to masturbate throughout life. It is estimated that about 95 percent of males masturbate, most often in adolescence, frequency declining with aging. Masturbation is also practiced occasionally even with a partner available. According to Kinsey, about 40 percent of women masturbate. Some start in late childhood, others in adolescence or adulthood. Female masturbation peaks in adulthood probably at ages thirty to forty.

How to Rate Yourself

Figure out your Sexual Quotient rating simply by adding up the number of times you circled T or F accurately:

HIGH: If you score twenty or more correct answers, your S.Q. is in the high zone, topping most other people by a sizable margin.

MODERATE: If you score from fifteen through nineteen correct answers, you have a moderate S.Q.—better than average.

AVERAGE OR LESS: If you score below fifteen correct answers, you have an average or lower S.Q.

It's heartening to know that with each page you read you'll expand your sexual knowledge and boost your S.Q. for future benefits. Educator Horace Mann stated it well: "Every addition to true knowledge is an addition to human power."

Now, with the specific how-to instructions provided, tied in with your practice and increasing proficiency with the Sexual Focus self-treatment technique, you'll be increasing your sexual "power." The following additional self-test will help move you in that positive direction.

Checklist of Most Prevalent Sexual Blocks

During the years of dealing with many patients, I have compiled a list of the fifteen most commonly expressed reasons many individuals, women and men, are not attaining and enjoying their full sexual potential. Understand that these are genuine explanations from many fine, "healthy" individuals, telling me why they don't find sex as fully satisfying as they expect or wish. Their goal was to get the *most* out of sex as an integral but not necessarily dominating part of their lives.

By checking this listing, you are taking a forthright, probing self test, and there's a very good chance that you'll track down personal blockages of which you may not have been clearly aware.

Are any of the following blocks affecting your sex life and general living negatively?

1. **Boredom** . . . "humdrum, dull, dreary, no fun."
2. **Routine** . . . "like operating a laundromat machine."
3. **Lack of imagination** . . . "no flights of fancy."
4. **Shyness** . . . "I can't help hiding inside myself."
5. **Passivity** . . . "I feel resigned, submissive, no spark."
6. **Fatigue** . . . "feel as wornout as an old shoe."
7. **Laziness** . . . "as sluggish as a swamp, that's me."
8. **Moral restrictions** . . . "I don't want to feel like a whore."
9. **Cultural restrictions** . . . "I have to maintain standards."
10. **Unawareness of alternatives** . . . "better sex . . . sure, but how?"

11. **Physical unsophistication . . .** "I just haven't been around."
12. **Self-consciousness . . .** "I can't put on a performance."
13. **Lack of communication** about sexual wants and desires.
14. **Reluctance to discuss** mutual physical responses.
15. **Other reasons . . .** think, identify and recognize your own, perhaps different, sexual blocks.

All these common blockages and others tend to limit the maximum sexual enjoyment available to almost everyone (probably including you). Through Erotic Focus, you will learn to recognize such hindrances through positive self-scrutiny. Then you can follow through with recommended self treatment which has worked beneficially for many others. By recognizing and overcoming such negative feelings, by opening up your mind and emotions, you'll profit from new sexual discoveries you may never have fully realized were possible for you.

2

MEASURE YOUR NATURAL E.F. APTITUDE; INSTANT EYE LOOK-UP TEST; PERSONAL ATTITUDES SELF-ANALYSIS QUIZ

Before I teach you the Erotic Focus technique, and show you how using it will improve your sexual enjoyment tremendously, you may be wondering whether it's a difficult technique to learn and to use. Put your mind at ease right now. Just about everyone has a natural E.F. aptitude, at least to a certain degree. The fact that you are showing your own keen interest by reading this book is confirmation that you are motivated to enjoy better sex. And that's extremely important. This beginning attitude points toward swift success in attaining that goal. E.F. makes use of the *inner resources* you already possess, which, concentrated through the Erotic Focus exercise, will enable you to apply greater sexual control, proficiency, and pleasure.

Here are two quick tests with which you can measure your E.F. aptitude:

1. Instant Eye Look-Up Test

In this first simple test, have your partner or a friend help you just by carefully watching the actions of your eyes gazing upward. The onlooker should note exactly how high your eyes rolled up, and compare your eyes with the drawings in the eye-action chart that follows.

NOTE: *For those of you who wear contact lenses, especially the hard lens variety, I advise that you take them out before you attempt to do the eye-roll "Look-Up" test. Hard contact lenses may dislocate, or make you feel uncomfortable.*

Instructions for taking this instant test. Look straight ahead. Now . . . keeping your head *in erect position* comfortably, roll your eyes up slowly, *eyelids staying wide open* . . . toward the top of your head, looking up and back as far as you can without straining. Have someone watch you and check on chart below how far your eyes rolled back, A-to-F.

Instant Eye Look-Up Test   Range

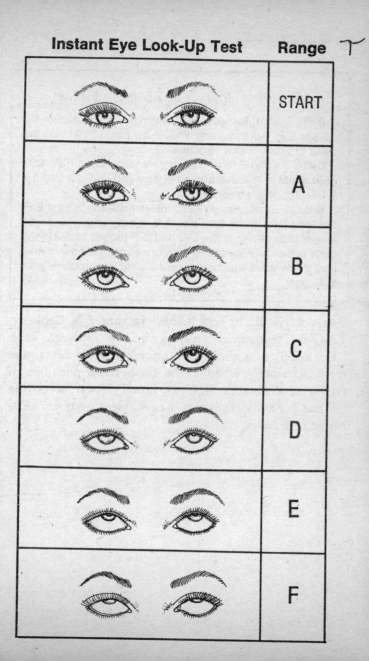

	Range
	START
	A
	B
	C
	D
	E
	F

Measuring Your "Eye Look-Up Range"

E-F . . . High-Range Responsiveness: You have an excellent E.F. Aptitude, and should be able to get into the state of Erotic Focus very quickly.

C-D . . . Mid-Range Responsiveness: Your E.F. aptitude starts in the average area, and you can get into the Erotic Focus state readily.

A-B . . . Lower-Range Responsiveness: Since your E.F. aptitude falls at the start into A-B, it may take you a little longer than others in the C-D and E-F ranges to attain the state of Sexual Focus. This merely means that it might take you a few extra practice sessions until you achieve your E.F. goal.

It's advisable to repeat the "Instant Eye Look-Up Test" a few times (resting briefly between each "Look-Up") so that your onlooker may determine most accurately whether the farthest-up positions of your eyeballs is at A, B, C, D, E or F. Then, according to that person's report, you can assess your personal range as follows:

Distribution of E.F. Float Capacity
as tested on over two thousand patients

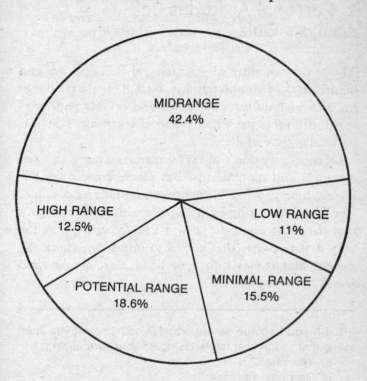

Whatever range you are in, you can be confident that you can shift voluntarily, and with full control, into the desired state of Erotic Focus and gain the many benefits. All you require is regular exercise with the E.F. technique to move to your highest individual potential. (Avoid extra straining; look up only to your own best level. With practice in E.F., you'll attain your utmost elevating feeling of buoyancy and relaxation.)

2. Personal Attitudes Self-Analysis Quiz

The second measure of your natural E.F. aptitude can be undertaken completely by yourself. It's a challenging self-analysis test that's fun and reveals your personal attitudes, personality and characteristics at this particular time of life.

Of course we don't always understand our own deep reactions and motivations, but please answer the following nine probing questions as candidly as possible. I've found in testing many people with similar quizzes that the most accurate answer usually surfaces in the very first response that comes to mind. So, check the answer that comes into your head most quickly and seems to fit you best.

---

1. Do you become so absorbed in doing something interesting that you almost totally disregard your surroundings?
   a) Yes, often.
   b) Only now and then.
   c) No, never.

2. In making important decisions, do you proceed basically with *logical reasoning* . . . or are you guided mostly by *instinctive feelings?*
   a) I always let my feelings guide me.
   b) Depends on the situation; sometimes I go by feelings, other times by logical reasoning.
   c) I always make logical decisions rather than depending on emotions and feelings.

3. In day-by-day activities, are you always intensely involved with what you're doing at the *present* . . . or do you usually consider *past* and *future* aspects?

    a) I always focus on the present.

    b) I consider a mixture of past, present and future aspects.

    c) I undertake present actions primarily in terms of past experiences and future consequences.

4. Do worries of the day influence your nighttime thoughts and activities overwhelmingly?

    a) No, I always turn off daytime worries so that they don't affect later activities negatively.

    b) I turn off my daytime concerns sometimes at night, but not always.

    c) I can't turn off daytime worries; I carry them with me and sound off into the night.

5. How do you rate your trust in other people, comparatively?

    a) Above average.

    b) Just about average.

    c) Below average—I'm very wary and suspicious.

6. When someone has to take control in a situation, do *you* prefer to take over, or have *someone else* take charge?

    a) I'd rather have someone else take charge.

    b) My attitude on who should take over depends on each particular situation.

    c) I always prefer to take control myself.

7. If you have a choice of *touching* or just *seeing* an object and/or a person, which course would give you more pleasure?

    a) I very much prefer to touch—I'm a toucher.

    b) I use both senses equally, touch and sight.

    c) I'm a visually oriented person; I prefer to look rather than touch.

In answering the next two test questions, please sit comfortably . . . or lie down on a couch or bed.

8. Close your eyes and imagine that your left or right hand has become so *heavy* that you can hardly lift or move it. How easy or difficult is this for you to imagine and do?

    a) I can do this very easily.

    b) It's not easy for me, but possible.

    c) I can't possibly do this.

9. Close your eyes again and imagine that your *whole body* feels very light and buoyant, as if floating in the air or on a cloud or on water. How easy is this for you to imagine and act out?

    a) I can do this very easily.

    b) I have to work hard on this, but it's possible.

    c) I can't possibly imagine or do this.

How to Figure Your E.F. Aptitude Rating

To arrive at your numerical score, count *five* for each "a" answer you've checked, count *three* for each of your "b" answers, count *one* for each "c" answer. Then add up all nine numbers you've checked—and the total is your personal score.

YOUR SCORE:

    30 to 45—High-Range E.F. Aptitude . . . you should be able to get into the state of Erotic Focus very quickly.

    20 to 29—Mid-Range E.F. Aptitude . . . your E.F. Aptitude starts in the avearage area, and you can get into the Erotic Focus state readily.

    9 to 19—Lower-Range E.F. Aptitude . . . since you start in the lower range, it may take you a little longer than others in the higher ranges to attain the state of Erotic Focus; you'll probably need a few extra practice sessions daily until you arrive at your target and use the E.F. technique most effectively.

Now compare your results in the *Look-Up Test* and the *Self-Analysis Quiz*. Combining your High-Range, Mid-Range, and Lower-Range "responsiveness" and "aptitude" assessments in both phases will show just about where you stand as you move on to learn and utilize the Erotic Focus Self-Treatment Method.

Keep in mind that these "scores" add up to a general assessment only of your E.F. aptitude. Consider this a probable guide to how many practice sessions you may require daily until you feel the results. Everyone should enjoy and get the benefits of at least three or four of the quick, mind-clearing, thought-concentrating E.F. breaks every day. You'll discover and profit from the proved E.F. gains for yourself. Your own E.F. experiences will be by far the most convincing demonstrations of the stimulating rewards you can attain.

3

LEARNING THE EROTIC FOCUS TECHNIQUE . . . STEP-BY-STEP

By following the simple step-by-step instructions accompanying the clear figure drawings here, you can begin your actual Erotic Focus exercises in minutes. With a little practice, you can start getting the benefits almost immediately. These are the exact same instructions which have helped thousands of my patients gain gratifying results and repeated, lasting rewards.

Please read the directions slowly and carefully as you practice the exercise step by step the first time. Then read and practice again, and again . . . going through the same motions as the figures in the drawings. After a few times, you will absorb and know the few steps easily—so that they become natural actions, like walking and talking.

As in learning anything else that will serve you for a lifetime, don't give up after the first time or two; if you don't quite understand fully at once, you will very soon. If you don't get into the delightful "E.F. float" in the first run-through, don't be at all discouraged. Many men and women have learned readily through my personal practice, lectures, and teaching in many settings *invariably in just one session*. You certainly will also.

In your E.F. float you can concentrate fully to get desired results. Just following the instructions will lead you quickly, smoothly and naturally into the pleasurable floating state, your thoughts free and released, which I call the "Erotic Focus Float." You will enjoy a new dimension of openness and eased inner control which gently sifts away harried and uptight feelings of stress and confusion. Most people don't lack the ability to concentrate; they simply don't know *how* to concentrate most effectively. In the E.F. state you *think* better, enabling you to *function* better.

I've always questioned the merit of the outmoded sign: "THINK." Most everyone can "think" (often without really thinking). However, you have the best chance to *accomplish* what you want when you learn how to direct and concentrate your thought processes toward a specific, desired result.

For instance, picture yourself in a second-story room just above the intersection of a very busy street. The windows are wide open and can't be closed. You begin trying to make love and to keep your mind on sex, or on something else that profits from total involvement. But loud traffic noises and the screaming of brakes and blaring of horns bombard you. Raucous noises from passing cars assault your ears and your consciousness. Thumping rock music is hammering through the thin walls from the neighbors' apartment . . .

In addition, personal conflicting concerns and questions are tumbling through your mind, such as: "Will I be able to handle that important client meeting tomorrow?" "Will I get a full throbbing erection?" "How can I take care of all those demanding relatives who are arriving for the weekend?" "Will I have an orgasm?" You're upset, disturbed, distracted.

When your mind is overloaded with conscious or unconscious stresses, problems, and disturbances, you clench up mentally, physically, and emotionally. Of course you can't function sexually (or any other way) at your peak. *You can clear away such confusions and doubts by going into your E.F. float.* Within seconds you begin easing and liberating your mind. You soon float alertly and buoyantly, lifted toward the fulfilling sexual pleasure you want.

Now, here's how easy it is to learn the E.F. float:

To begin, select a time and place for relative privacy. If you wear contact lenses, always remove them before rolling your eyes up. The E.F. exercise may be done either sitting in a comfortable armchair or lying on a couch or bed—whatever suits you personally, whatever is most relaxing and comforting. You are beginning a pleasurable, rewarding experience—*enjoy it.*

NOTE: *Read through the instructions first, perhaps several times, as needed, before you practice the steps. It's vital that you thoroughly understand how to enter the state of Erotic Focus, then how to end each session when you please before you actually go through the whole procedure. For reference, you may wish to refer to chart on pages 00-00.*

Step 1: If you are sitting up, keep your head straight but not stiff and look directly ahead in a relaxed position.

If you are lying down, rest your head comfortably

against the horizontal surface, and look straight up at the ceiling, feeling at ease and unpressured. Your eyes should focus easily on the ceiling, without any strong fixation or strain.

Step 2: Hold your head in the comfortable straight-ahead position, sitting or lying down. (If wearing contact lenses, remove them.) Now roll your eyes up and back, trying to look up past your eyebrows and right over the top and back of your head. (Don't strain, just roll the eyeballs up and back as far as you can comfortably.)

Step 3: Continue to look up and over and back, and now, as you are looking over and back, close your eyelids s-l-o-w-l-y (**still** feeling that you are keeping your eyes rolled back, but never with any strain or discomfort).

Step 4: Maintaining the eyelids-closed state, now take a deep breath through your nose, mouth closed and keep breathing in deeply, deeply (but never straining) . . . and hold your breath for some seconds (according to your personal capacity, never overexerting).

Step 5: Then . . . slowly exhale through your slightly opened lips, and while you are exhaling, keeping your eyelids closed for this entire step . . . let your eyes come down, back into their normal straight-ahead position.

Note: *As you breathe in and out deeply, think inhaling good feelings . . . exhaling tension.*

Step 6: Now . . . still with your eyelids closed . . . feeling very good, peaceful and pleasant . . . breathing easily at your normal rate . . . *imagine your* *entire body is sinking deeper and deeper into the chair, couch or bed* . . . so relaxed, feeling so benign . . . as you enjoy the delightful floating sensation of Erotic Focus. (In E.F., you are both fully eased in mind and body and, at the same time, uplifted and alert. The result is a delicious floating sensation.)

Step 7: Enjoy this feeling of airiness . . . and now shift your attention to focus gently on your right or left hand, as you choose . . . and imagine hand and arm, from hand to elbow, becoming very light and quite weightless . . . letting your hand and lower arm float upward slowly and easily and naturally (bending at the elbow, fingers and hand limp) . . .

Step 8: You have reached your goal . . . as your hand and arm have floated upward easily to the upright position noted in the picture, elbow resting on the arm of the chair or surface of the couch. You are now experiencing the desired, pleasurable state of Erotic Focus. Keep your eyes closed . . . mind and body floating, fully at ease. *Your arm will remain pleasantly and effortlessly in this bent-upright position during the entire E.F. period, unless the directions advise you otherwise.*

This eight-step simple procedure, going along from step to step easily—and without any feeling of pressure or urgency whatsoever—will occupy only about twenty seconds once you have learned the progression thoroughly. You achieve the sequence smoothly and easily. At first it may take you a little longer, but just go along at the pace which is most comfortable and unpressured for you personally. You may proceed with the method more slowly if that suits you better.

It is desirable that you practice and train yourself to

enter the state of Erotic Focus in as short a time as possible comfortably for yourself. Thus, when you start using the E.F. technique to help treat and solve your specific problem in the future, it is advantageous, naturally, to get in and out of the state as automatically as possible.

The length of time you spend on each occasion in the E.F. state will depend on the particular treatment strategy you use (see next chapter). Even though it can take as little as twenty seconds to enter E.F., you may remain in E.F. for more seconds or minutes . . . according to what you feel you need to bring about the desired result, as you will learn.

Now, once you have attained the pleasant Erotic Focus float, your body will be enjoying a wonderfully restful feeling of beneficial relaxation, while your mind, freed of the usual pressures and tensions, is clear and alert, not dulled or sleepy.

Using Erotic Focus for Personal Benefit

For a little while, in the desired state of Erotic Focus, simply let your mind remain in neutral gear. That means keeping your mind "idling," relaxed, at peace, not concentrating on anything specific, just floating restfully, preferably with your eyes closed loosely, never squeezed tight, never frowning with strain. It is vital that you acquire the ability to float your mind pleasurably this special E.F. way, without mental or physical tension.

As you realize now, eliminating intrusive pressures is an important part of solving and overcoming many sexual dysfunctions, problems and other barriers. It is certainly well established professionally that anxiety and stress are frequently prime contributors to sexual problems or concerns, and may trigger serious dysfunctions.

While you are in the wonderfully relaxed state of Erotic Focus, your mind is "open" and now extraordinarily responsive, probably as never before, to new attitudes, information and approaches which will then be conveyed to your unconscious mind. With E.F., your instructions to yourself will be able to penetrate your consciousness relatively unimpeded, unblocked, like a revealing beam of laser light. The result is clear focus, insight and understanding. You will then be responsive to your own new productive *imprint* made possible in your mind with the E.F. technique.

All this will lead you to adopt a different, essential, beneficial point of view in pursuing your activities for the ultimate sexual fulfillment you seek. You will gain a new approach, *relief from constrictions imposed on yourself by yourself unconsciously*.

For your better understanding, let's compare the human brain, your brain in this case, to a computer which you will learn how to make ready to "operate." Your "brain computer" will be operated only by you. It will be in your charge always, prepared to receive instructions which you, in full knowledgeable control, are about to feed into it. Through the preceding steps by which you will have achieved the state of E.F. readiness, you will have prepared your mind to move forward for the gains and successes you want and need.

Understand this: the human mind, your mind, is the best, most efficient and productive personal computer. It can provide the top proficiency in aiding to attain your own maximum sexual enjoyment and performance in most instances—once you know how to "program" and use it in your own behalf—through the simple E.F. technique you learn here.

Once you are in the state of Erotic Focus (a mechanical computer might flash the signal: "E.F. ready"), your personal "brain computer" is all set for you to insert some new, productive programming leading to the desired result. You are ready and able to erase old blocking, perhaps misleading and thus damaging responses. Then you can feed in new directions and attitudes.

After you feed the new, corrective instructions and essential information into your receptive "brain computer," you will have accomplished what is required. Your better new course will have been established deeply in your mind. You are all set for the new, fruitful effect you require and desire—the solution you have sought.

You'll learn how to apply remedial self-treatment for personal situations in detail in the following chapter.

Right now, briefly, here's how to bring yourself out of the self-induced state of Erotic Focus at any instant that you decide to do so. Remember, you are in full control of yourself throughout the entire E.F. exercise.

Emerging From E.F.

Once you have "programmed" your "brain computer," as instructed in entering the state of E.F.—and put into effect the remedial directions (see next chapter) for your problem—you bring yourself out of the Erotic Focus float very easily and pleasantly. There is no problem whatsoever—you are in charge every second—there is no mystery or magic about E.F.

What you will be doing, as you will note, is *reversing* the process of *entering* the state of Erotic Focus, as you now bring yourself back to your personal "normal" situation where you started. When you emerge quickly and without strain or pressure, you will feel eased and refreshed, definitely better than when you began.

Simply proceed as follows (reversing the steps used in entering E.F.):

Step 1R (for "Return"): Your eyelids are still closed. Now, again, take a deep breath through your nose, keeping your mouth closed, holding your breath for a moment comfortably, never straining or overexerting yourself . . .

Step 2R: As you are inhaling (in Step 1R), eyelids closed, and then holding your breath . . . with your eyes back up under your closed eyelids, rolling as far up and back as you can without stress . . .

Step 3R: Exhale slowly through your mouth, pursing your lips a bit so air escapes gradually . . . and while the air is being breathed out, open your eyelids s-l-o-w-l-y . . .

Step 4R: Easily, pleasantly, feeling relaxed and rested . . . eyes open . . . let your straight-ahead gaze come back into clear focus . . .

Step 5R: Open and close the hand which is still in the upright position . . . repeat opening and closing the hand slowly and comfortably, no clenching . . . doing this a few times . . .

Step 6R: Slowly, without any force or tension, let your elevated hand and arm return gently back down to its normal resting position . . .

Step 7R: Stay in the sitting or lying position for

some leisurely seconds . . . looking straight forward at the start . . . then look about you. Now you can proceed with your activities again, as you wish. You'll feel exceptionally refreshed and at ease, with enhanced inner vitality and freedom from stress.

Three Special E.F. "Plus" Tips

1. In the process of entering the state of E.F., a number of my patients have found it helpful to keep repeating to themselves slowly and silently the two initials "E.F. . . . E.F. . . . E.F. . . ."

2. Some enthusiasts tell me that it helps them get into the E.F. float fast to *visualize in the mind's eye the E.F. initials large,* as if cut out of wood, floating in space.

3. Other patients have said that they were helped to get into the E.F. float, and increase the benefits, by repeating the words "Erotic Focus" to themselves slowly, silently, drawing out the second word by lingering on the "oh" sound this way: "Erotic Foh-h-h-cus," extending the "ohhh" in quiet concentration.

While not essential to the Erotic Focus technique, you too may find one or both of these extra little devices a very pleasant, supportive aid in attaining E.F. and its benefits swiftly and surely. You may wish to use these two "plusses" generally or occasionally or not at all, in order to achieve the Erotic Focus float most effectively. I suggest that you try them and decide for yourself.

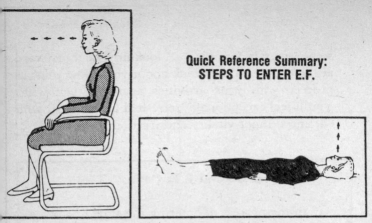

**Quick Reference Summary:
STEPS TO ENTER E.F.**

Sit in an armchair or lie down on a couch or bed, eyes straight ahead.

2. Roll your eyes way up and back.

3. Keeping your eyes looking up, close your eyelids slowly.

4. Take a deep breath through your nose, hold for a few seconds.

5. Slowly exhale through slightly opened lips, letting your eyes roll back down under closed eyelids.

6. Imagine your body sinking deeper and deeper into the chair or couch. ►

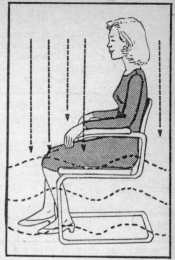

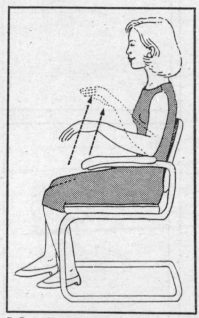

7. Eyes still closed, focus your mind on your right or left hand, let your hand and arm become light and float upward.

8. Keep your eyes closed, elbow resting on the arm of chair or surface of couch, enjoying the state of Erotic Focus. ▼

Quick Reference Summary:
STEPS TO EMERGE FROM E.F.

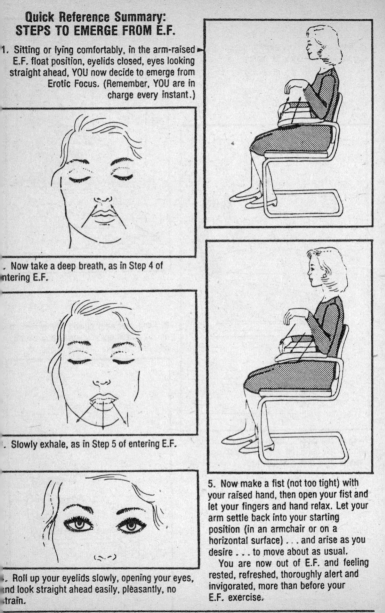

1. Sitting or lying comfortably, in the arm-raised E.F. float position, eyelids closed, eyes looking straight ahead, YOU now decide to emerge from Erotic Focus. (Remember, YOU are in charge every instant.)

. Now take a deep breath, as in Step 4 of entering E.F.

. Slowly exhale, as in Step 5 of entering E.F.

. Roll up your eyelids slowly, opening your eyes, and look straight ahead easily, pleasantly, no strain.

5. Now make a fist (not too tight) with your raised hand, then open your fist and let your fingers and hand relax. Let your arm settle back into your starting position (in an armchair or on a horizontal surface) . . . and arise as you desire . . . to move about as usual.

You are now out of E.F. and feeling rested, refreshed, thoroughly alert and invigorated, more than before your E.F. exercise.

NOTE: If you don't bring yourself out of E.F. this way, it will leave naturally with sleep, or whenever you wish. . . . **YOU** are always in charge.

How to Take a Quickie "E.F. Relaxation Break" Anywhere, Anytime

There are many times during the day or at night when you feel somewhat uptight, perhaps tense, and have the need or desire to ease up, unwind and get your thoughts together, or, as the saying goes, "get my head together." You can do just that quickly almost anytime and anywhere with a quickie E.F. Relaxation Break.

It's very easy to do that with the E.F. self-treatment exercise when sitting or lying down, as taught in the preceding pages. Also, happily, you can get the Erotic Focus lift without attracting notice wherever you are—standing on a corner waiting for a bus . . . sitting on a bus or parked in a car . . . in an auditorium, during a movie or TV show . . . when and as you wish. Here's how . . .

Many of my patients call this the "camouflage exercise." There are just two simple changes from the regular E.F. exercise: First, as you are—standing or sitting or even lying on the beach—*close* your eyes for a few seconds, and roll your eyes up as in the usual Step 2 but *under your closed eyelids.* That makes it completely private—no one sees your eyes directed way up and back.

Now, with your eyes looking up and back behind your closed eyelids, take a deep breath . . . hold it for a few seconds . . . then exhale and let your eyes roll back down to the natural straight-ahead position behind your closed eyelids . . .

As you feel your mind easing and relaxing, bringing you mental and physical unwinding and relief, let your hand come up and touch your forehead as though you're in deep thought, just as people tend to do often at a table or desk, and when standing and waiting.

All this takes about twenty seconds, and during that brief time you shift gears, establish the extra E.F. receptivity and focus on clearing your mind of stress and disturbing thoughts. Then you shift back out again by lowering your hand and opening your eyes. Your head will be cleared and you can go back to your work or whatever you are undertaking. You will be thinking better and acting more efficiently and effectively due to renewed alertness and energy after E.F.

By doing this "camouflage exercise" when it's more appropriate, or the regular E.F. exercise when you are alone—time after time—you are establishing a *private signal system*. This little E.F. quickie exercise helps you stay alert and refreshed for any commitment. It all takes so little time and proceeds so naturally that no one else will notice, but you will get a calming and reenergizing E.F. lift.

Please understand the very special self-power and self-control you have with the Erotic Focus Self-Treatment Method, unique among most mind-relaxing techniques: *You move in and out of the E.F. float at will,* as you gain both an easing and alerting of your true mental powers, alleviating common stress and pressures.

You now understand how to go into the E.F. state, and remain as short or long a time as you wish. You can enjoy the E.F. float for only a minute or so if that's all you desire for the quick beneficial effect—and out again, as you will it. Or you can stay in for a longer time, even into the night if you are in bed and going to sleep. The helpful E.F. effect will evaporate as you sleep or whenever you let it drift away.

Thus, even when you use the quickie E.F. method in a situation where you lack privacy, you will find it remarkably refreshing and reenergizing. E.F. always instills a pleasurable sense of clarifying repose.

The more often you take a twenty-second E.F. "break" each day, the regular exercise or the quickie camouflage exercise, the more you will become profitably free from negative stress. I recommend up to ten E.F. breaks during waking hours, especially at the start. Your mind and concentration will be released to focus unrestrained attention toward achieving your desired goals. This applies to sex but also to all of your daily living.

On to Supersex in Your E.F. State

Here's another clear example to help you understand the extra released self-power you get in the state of Erotic Focus focused concentration:

Think of those most productive periods when you were doing something that absorbed you totally, something you cared very much about doing. For instance, you might have been writing a long, important letter to a close friend, reporting a complicated series of critical happenings in detail. Or you might be concentrating on entering and solving an intricate tax problem. Or you might be listening breathlessly to a magnetic lecturer explaining a complex scientific dilemma, as you applied closest attention to understand fully.

Do you remember how completely involved you were for that period of time? Your mind was cleared of any other thoughts or stresses that might have distracted you from your particular focal point. You shut out any distractions, permitting nothing to sidetrack your attention.

The Erotic Focus float works similarly in respect to your functioning when preparing for and having sex with a partner. Obtrusive thoughts, pressures, stresses of all kinds which might interrupt and interfere are cleared away. You are mentally, emotionally and physically free.

Thus, in the focused concentration of your self-induced, purposeful E.F. state, your participation and functioning are directed totally upon getting the greatest pleasure and fulfillment from sex and closeness between your partner and yourself.

Through the Erotic Focus technique, you can get all the benefits conveyed to you in the information and recommendations you will find throughout this book by reading it all carefully. Doubts, worries, uncertainties, and inhibitions tend to ease off automatically and pleasantly. There's never any strain in the E.F. state. Read on to find out how to proceed and apply yourself in sexual participation for most satisfying and most prolonged enjoyment.

4

USING EROTIC FOCUS TO COMMUNICATE AND CONNECT

For the most gratifying and fulfilling sexual intercourse, partners must develop an effective communication system. You'll learn here exactly how to use your sexual focus ability for the better communication that can mean fullest sexual rewards.

First, learn to share feelings to develop a sense of closeness and intimacy, to understand and be understood. Lack of communication has been described as "a horrible feeling that nobody's listening," and it can mean that sex becomes an empty experience instead of a joyous one. But it's a two-way street: (a) You must express your thoughts and emotions clearly and (b) your partner must listen attentively and respond in ways that show full understanding of what you've described.

Without that lucid two-way communication, you never really know what the other person is thinking and feeling. And no matter how close you feel to your partner, he or she can't *guess* what you are thinking and feeling. You must *tell* them. Only then can the two of you connect most deeply and fully. I've seen unhappy people transformed into ecstatic lovers once they learn how to turn the key that opens the door to *full two-way communication*.

Learning to Talk About Sex

Here's an instructive example from my practice: Laurie was referred by her doctor for therapy because she'd become depressed due to unhappiness in her marriage. She told me, "After five years, I feel sexually unfulfilled. I don't enjoy making love. My husband, Ben, goes right at it. No foreplay. He just inserts his penis. He comes, turns away, and then switches on the TV to watch a late-night movie."

She paused, then went on, "I've tried to talk with him. But he just grunts or turns away without a real response. So I've given up. I became furious, then depressed. It's hopeless."

"Don't you ever talk to each other?" I asked.

"Oh, yes . . ." she said slowly. "I know that communication is important in any relationship, so I try. We're able to talk about everything else openly. Yet when it comes to *sex,* I can't get one word out of Ben." She hesitated. "I'm shy about it too. I just can't open up—nor can he."

"You're not the only one who finds it difficult to talk to your husband about sex, or vice versa," I explained. "Our so-called free and open society is far from that when it comes to expressing personal sexual feelings. I'm still amazed to see people who have shared their lives and their bodies for many years, but aren't able to put sexual matters into words. Verbal communication is extremely important, especially if there is something that *needs* to be said. Nobody can read the other's thoughts. Now, *here's what to do.*"

These instructions worked for Laurie and Ben, and can for you: Use the Erotic Focus method to clarify your thoughts. Go into the state of E.F. Then "rehearse" carefully what you want to tell your partner. You might begin with very neutral, easy statements such as: "We've been making love all these years, but I've never told you that I really like to feel your hot, hard penis inside of me."

Yes, speak right out—calmly, but directly to the point. He may be stunned, but he won't be displeased. So go on: "How does it feel to you when you come?" Then, perhaps, "You know I would enjoy it if you could once make me climax by going down on me."

Now, after you've examined this a few times in E.F. in your mind—even anticipating your partner's reactions—you'll find it much easier to do it in real life. It's worth trying, isn't it? It will open up both of you for a new dimension of better sex.

"Then do this," I told Laurie. "Suggest that Ben go through this book and read your penciled notes on some items that are especially pertinent to both of you, such as the recommendations here on communicating. That makes it easy to ask him, 'Did you get a chance to look at the passages I marked for you? What about trying such-and-such tonight?' "

It's easy once you get started, and you can get wonderful results. Silence does *not* bring the best sexual connection. Clarify your thoughts and desires in E.F., then put them into words. *Speak out*.

Communicating to Solve Problems

These days when most individuals, women and men, work hard in demanding careers and jobs, it's vital for each to be able to sound off, to handle and help solve stressful individual work problems that often interfere with satisfying sexual functioning in the relationship. Recently I saw a couple, Peter and Pauline, who were living together and enjoyed "great sex" until the last few months.

Pauline said, "We started to avoid sex for weeks at a time. We were each having hard times at work, felt frustrated, irritable and fearful about the job future, but kept it all boiling inside us—"

Peter interrupted, "I tried to approach Pauline several times, to talk about my problems on the job. But she'd cut me off, saying something like, 'Come on, you have nothing to worry about. At least you have job security, they can't fire you from your civil service work. But I'm so worried about my new boss not liking me and that he'll just fire me . . .' "

"That's true," Pauline insisted. "I am worried."

Peter said, "Sure . . . but I feel squelched. So I get angry, slam doors and yell about her messiness, leaving clothes around, silly stuff like that. By the time we go to bed, we're both so upset that sex is out of the question."

It's clear what went wrong with their communication system: Whenever Peter tried to tell Pauline about his job problems, she wouldn't listen. When she wanted to talk about feeling exploited at work, he wouldn't respond because she'd tell him how much better off he was and that she was the one who needed support. Thus, they both felt rejected, not understood.

Here's the significant point: If one could have delayed the need for comfort and timed it differently, then each speak up in turn, both would enjoy needed understanding and support. They would move together toward helpful solutions and resultant loving sexual release and pleasure so vital in any relationship.

It's really so simple, isn't it? Just *focus* on the communication need and goal. If one partner is trying to express feelings, and the other is seeking to solve a problem, and neither lets the other speak out urgently, both end up feeling angry, bottled up. With that *mis*communication at one level, the sexual level is bound to be harmfully affected.

"It's bad enough when one partner brings aggravation and work stress to bed," I told Peter and Pauline. "It's far worse when you both do. Remember this: *Keeping up a sexual relationship is especially needed when you're both having work or other problems*. Sex not only makes one feel good but also functions to release tension, anxiety and stress. Don't miss out on this marvelous natural mechanism to relieve tensions built up over the day. It's unfair and destructive to take it out on each other."

I instructed them carefully, and now you: *Here's what you do:* Every evening as soon as you come home, go into the E.F. float, and shift gears. Project all the unpleasant things on a screen. Leave the negatives there while your body starts to relax.

"Now, imagine anything you can think of that helps you feel good, such as a trip you took together. Relive happy incidents and memories. Repeat this E.F. exercise right before going to bed. You might recall thrilling, loving sexual scenes together, then reach out, speak up, make love. Keep in mind, always, whatever the external pressures, the more openly and freely you communicate your thoughts and feelings, the less any outside adversity will affect you and the better your sex life will be."

Changing "Untouchable" into "Touchable"

One can and must learn how to open up and disclose feelings and needs to a partner. Even people with deep-seated sexual problems that involve lack of communication have been able to overcome them with the help of E.F. Quite often *tactile*, that is, physical touching, as well as *verbal* relating is involved.

Stop a moment here to ask yourself, "Am I communicating fully through caressing, stroking, fondling?" These are among the most exciting pleasures of sexual intercourse, yet are not used often enough by people. The tingling skin surface itself, the arousing sense of touching and being embraced and cuddled, contribute to great erotic enjoyment. These bonuses should never be neglected if you are to experience the most thrilling stimulaton, fulfillment and rapport.

Doris and Tom, in their midtwenties, visited me when they'd been married almost two years after living together for a year. They had a good sexual relationship, they felt, with just one disruptive flaw—Doris didn't like to be fondled. Mostly she resisted having her breasts and nipples touched and caressed. She said she found that contact extremely unpleasant. Concerns such as these are quite common.

Tom had accepted this initially, but after a year of marriage began complaining bitterly. He insisted that fondling a woman's breasts really turned him on. He resented being denied that special gratification by his wife. Her gynecologist had examined Doris thoroughly, and said there was no apparent physical reason for the reported breast discomfort.

"I can't stand Doris pushing my hands away and sometimes even wearing her bra to conceal her beautiful breasts when we're making love," Tom grumbled. "After all, I am her husband!"

She protested, "You didn't complain until lately. I'm beginning to get sick of your whining, and of your penis getting soft inside me—"

"That's only because you won't let me feel your tits and stroke your nipples," he erupted angrily. "No wonder I lose my erection!"

Doris revealed, after detailed discussion, that when she was only twelve and first developing breasts, her sixteen-year-old brother had squeezed her breasts at every possible chance, and hurt her. She had buried the memory. But now when her breasts were touched she felt guilty, as though she had done something dirty. So she hated to be touched there at any time.

I taught them both the Erotic Focus method, and explained that in the E.F. relaxed state she'd lose her fears. She would realize clearly now, I emphasized, that she was not to blame for something her brother had done to her. She would understand, thinking about it clearly in a mature way, that such childhood experiences were quite common. She would recognize the difference between Tom's motivation for touching as an expression of his love and affection for her, as compared with the aggressive, violent invasion of her body by her older brother.

I pointed out to Tom that in the clarified state of E.F., he'd be aware of Doris's feelings and reactions. Thus, he'd be more gentle, knowing her deep-seated reluctance to have her breasts caressed. He'd now understand too that some women feel sore and tender in the breasts and nipples shortly before they menstruate.

Furthermore, he would realize in his newly aware state that Doris probably had to be deeply aroused sexually *before* she could enjoy having her breasts fondled. In E.F. he could take his time, stroking and exploring other parts of her body until she was wet and very excited. Then he could assist in encouraging her to guide his hand to her breasts when she was ready.

It became clear to both of them that he had developed his own "power failure" due to emotional rather than physical reasons. He'd been losing erections because he felt rejected by her. And each time her hands pushed him away, his resentment and resultant anxiety about performing had magnified to the point of impotence.

I told them both to do the Erotic Focus exercise a number of times daily, separately, not just when having sex. This would aid personal relaxation and clarity of thinking. In the buoyant, serene state, each could reflect individually on enjoying sex without fear of pain on her part, or impotence in his case. In the E.F. float, each could focus on the good aspects of their relationship and think of sex as an expression of love and affection, not a battleground for power and pain.

With the help of E.F., they overcame their problems within a short time. They reported to me a while later that they'd been enjoying ecstatic and fulfilling sex ever since. Now sexually content and at ease, they were able to communicate effectively, and "talk it out" lovingly, as I'd urged. They said they'd become much closer than ever before.

How E.F. Aids Communication

As you talk things through, you undergo what can be compared to what is known professionally as "systematic desensitization." Don't let the strange-sounding phrase put you off. "Systematic" here simply means step-by-step advancement as you open up your thoughts and your feelings. "Desensitization" means that you relieve and reduce uncertainty, fear, sorrow, emotional pain and suffering.

Use of the Erotic Focus technique by Doris and Tom, plus thinking and talking about the problem with each other "systematically desensitized" Doris about any guilt due to her brother touching her breasts in her teen years. Thus she progressed to welcoming and thoroughly enjoying having Tom fondle her breasts and nipples. That "extra," plus better communication and understanding, added greatly to their mutual sexual pleasure.

Similarly, Tom dropped his feelings of resentment and inadequacy, as touching his wife anywhere and everywhere became for both a free and natural expression, a source of enhanced pleasure. What had been an increasingly immovable barrier in their relationship was now a stimulus to their closeness and unqualified love and loving. The case of Doris and Tom shows how you can profit similarly from better communication through E.F. to help get rid of any sexual hangups of your own.

Why are people afraid to speak up? Sometimes we are afraid to ask the partner for something specific out of fear of being rejected. Most people need to feel sure that their wants and needs will be accepted and respected. Acceptance doesn't necessarily mean that one partner agrees with what the other wants, but at least knows about it and has the chance to understand and act accordingly.

If there's a conflict between different opinions of the two partners, but they accept each other's differences, then they're on the way to a solution. Possible ways should be discussed until both agree on a final compromise. Then, use a trial period to work it out. This way each person can avoid blaming the other, and neither can be made to feel guilty any time later.

In communication there is understanding and strengthening of love and sexual fulfillment. Therefore it is very important to learn and follow through on the checkpoints which follow. My time-proven Erotic Focus technique can help by targeting just where the communication has gone astray. Then you have the knowledge to restructure your communication system for the results you want and need.

5-Point Checklist of Sexual Communication Skills

1. Communicate in many available ways: Verbal (talk) . . . visual (sight) . . . tactile (touch) . . . auditory (hearing) . . . olfactory (sense of smell). All are significant individually or together. Sometimes a close hug (tactile) can convey more than a hundred words. Shakespeare noted that "a golden touch could soften steel and stone"—and human flesh. A long, passionate glance between two people may unite more deeply than a discussion about love. Listening intently to your lover's voice, smelling the warm fragrance of trembling skin—all intensify sensuality.

But always consider transmitting your feelings in words. If you say nothing, you convey nothing, and an opportunity for maximum intimacy is lost.

2. Speak in a neutral not dictatorial manner. Avoid sounding off too strongly, conveying that you are right and any other view is wrong. That sparks controversy, not communication. For example, if you are sure that your partner is overspending on clothes to look most sexy and desirable, think before you accuse. You might ask pleasantly, "I wonder, is some of the money spent on clothes cutting in on our vacation fund?"

That's a "neutral" statement, compared with, "You're spending too damn much on sexy clothes.

What are you trying to prove?'' That's accusatory, inviting an angry, defensive retort and erecting a block against sexual joining. On the other hand, a gentle question encouraging a reasonable explanation would more likely lead to an understanding, loving embrace.

3. Seek to build up, not tear down. Beware using words as destructive weapons that demean the other person, diminishing sexual self-esteem and confidence. If you feel neglected and hurt, try to connect rather than accuse. Avoid blurting out, ''I'll bet you can't even get it up anymore!'' It makes a world of difference if you reach out instead to touch and kiss and suggest softly, ''Let's talk about it . . .''

4. Search out the truth, avoid impulsive reactions. How often have you responded negatively to something your partner says, then realized too late that you started a controversy because you didn't first find the facts? As a result, sexual closeness was destroyed, temporarily or permanently.

For instance, arriving home very late, he explains, ''I'm sorry, I was tied up in a tough office meeting. I couldn't call or leave until I got my point across.'' Hurt, angry because of waiting, you erupt, ''You're lying—you were tied up with your gorgeous secretary!'' The next day you learn from someone else that the meeting did run late. You apologize, but you lost a night of lovemaking, and you've caused a split between you.

I suggest that you take a quickie E.F. break first. Consider the situation in the clarifying E.F. state. Then speak up calmly. You're not likely to find truth or harmony in a storm of angry words.

5. Above all, strive for clear, mutual understand-

ing. A very common error among couples is that they don't communicate their thoughts and desires clearly and directly. Too often one or the other assumes, "He ought to know by now . . ." But he *doesn't* know. Wrong assumptions ruin many relationships. Why take something for granted—sexual doubts or suspicions or anything else—when open, direct interchange can reveal the truth?

Clearing up Confusion Through Communication

Very often the solution to an aggravating sexual problem can be found simply by speaking out, asking, telling. Here's a clear illustration: Holly visited me because she feared that her marriage and herself were near a breakdown . . .

In her twenties, Holly was terribly confused about her deteriorating live-in relationship with Roy. "I still love him," she said, "and I'm sure he loves me, but our sex life is awful. He's a lousy lover. He never brings me to orgasm; I'm never sexually satisfied."

Through discussion it came out that "I need to be stroked all over. My skin is very sensitive and the touching arouses me. But Roy seems to think caressing is a waste of time." Suddenly she burst out, "I met another man who knows how to please me. He touches and kisses me all over, fondles and licks my breasts and—uh—genitals until I come again and again just from the prolonged pressure and tonguing . . ."

She paused, then continued, "He's not really my type,

but I may be falling in love with him because he fulfills me sexually. Roy is intelligent and caring, but . . . I don't know what to do, I'm so confused . . . *I want to be satisfied sexually!*'' She paused. ''What's wrong with me?''

I assured her, ''There is nothing 'wrong' with you. You're right, the skin is an important part of sexual arousal. Being touched all over is an essential of most exciting lovemaking. Primarily, I believe that what is missing between you and Roy is *communication*.

''Think it through,'' I suggested. ''If you love each other, why go to someone else to get what you're missing at home? Have you ever tried to convey your wants and desires openly? Give it a trial—*speak out*. Learn the Erotic Focus method, and encourage Roy to do so. While in E.F., practice caressing each other all over tenderly, lovingly, passionately. You'll both expand your sexual repertoire excitingly. You'll get what you need from each other, and won't desire outside affairs.''

After a couple of visits, a radiant Holly told me, ''Our sex is glorious, far more fulfilling with Roy than with the other man, because our love multiplies our passion.'' She shook her head, added with a bewildered laugh, ''It turns out that Roy enjoys touching and being stroked too, but thought that I didn't. We could have made it clear so easily just by trusting each other and speaking up.''

The best way to arrive at mutual understanding and desired change is to be specific and to the point in expressing yourself. Be direct: ''I wish you'd caress me all over, including my genitals. It makes me feel so good, I love you even more.'' The alternative of saying nothing—the mistake Holly and Roy made of being silent and passive—can destroy your relationship.

5

LOVEMAKING THROUGH EROTIC FOCUS

FOUR BASIC PHASES OF SEXUAL INTERCOURSE

Phase I—DESIRE . . . originates in the brain.

Phase II—EXCITEMENT . . . primarily physical/genital/vascular functioning.

Phase III—ORGASM . . . genital/muscular reflexes.

Phase IV—RESOLUTION . . . after-orgasm responses.

You will benefit from understanding each of the four basic phases of sexual intercourse, and how you personally experience each phase. This knowhow can lead you to improved sexual functioning and enjoyment as you use E.F. to help fulfill your own needs and to get maximum pleasure from each phase.

Phase I—Desire (libido): Sexual desire is the wish or appetite for sex and like all human drives such as hunger, thirst, and the need to sleep is initiated in the brain. When you feel desire, you become receptive to sexual encounters—you are sexually aroused; in the vernacular: "horny." The desire phase is probably the most dominating aspect of human sexuality.

Without desire, sex can be unpleasant, even injurious. Depression, excess pressure, fear, insecurity, and in the extreme form—rape—all can inhibit or kill desire. Such lack of desire may extend for long periods. A large percentage of people—women more than men—get exceptional pleasure from the desire phase. During the courting time, Phase I is especially intense, filled with accelerating desire. Savoring the desire phase fully and getting the most out of it is essential for you to get greatest enjoyment from the three oncoming phases.

Phase II—Excitement: This phase teems with physical evidences—swelling and moistening of the labia in the female, and engorgement of the penis in the male. Utmost sexual pleasure from this phase can be expanded by preparation with the E.F. technique. Case histories will instruct you on just how to get the most gratification from this excitement stage.

Phase III—Orgasm: For many, this is the payoff of the sexual act—the overwhelming orgastic sensations. Enhanced by E.F. aliveness, contraction of the pelvic muscles in the female, and emission and ejaculation stages in the male of Phase III can produce optimum thrills for both partners—in simultaneous or separate orgasms.

Phase IV—Resolution: This stage, after sexual intercourse has occurred, can be most rewarding of all. Unfortunately, not everyone realizes this and makes the most of the possibilities. Extraordinary physical, emotional, and mental reactions are possible in both females and males, and those who make the most of deepened feelings available through aroused consciousness and aided by E.F. increased awareness can gain immediate and enduring *extra* rewards.

Enough time should be devoted to calming down, relaxing deeply and slowly to a more "normal" level, while enjoying every sensation. Each partner should enfold and gently caress the other, making the most of the intimate and loving feelings you experience during this time. This relaxed period is perfect for exchanging tender words, for touching one another in most fulfilling ways. This is potentially the most meaningful aspect of sexual relations— when you are informed and aware enough to make it so. You can fulfill to the utmost the basic human need for attachment to another.

All four phases of sexual intercourse can be enhanced and made more responsive through learning and using the Erotic Focus Method.

Gaining the Utmost in Sexual Fulfillment from Each Phase

Now that you understand the four basic phases of the sexual response, take a moment to ask yourself which phase *you* personally enjoy most now—one or more or all. Which one or more should you improve to benefit you most? All four can be enhanced by learning and using the Erotic Focus method. To help yourself most, do the following:

Step 1: Go into the E.F. state. Now, floating pleasurably aware, very alert and in command, imagine that you are looking at a screen—a TV screen, movie screen, or just a blank wall . . .

On this screen, project the moving details of your last sexual experience. Reproduce the entire sequence of that most recent sexual intercourse . . . and just let it roll in front of your eyes across this imaginary screen . . .

Examine the scene critically and most attentively (remember, your senses are heightened in E.F. so you are better able to scrutinize, to understand, to assess). You may even stop the "film" here and there, and just zoom in on specific happenings, as you please. Dwell on each, then go on to another occasion of sexual intercourse, and perhaps another. Keep in mind what you learn from purposeful, searching scrutiny of each phase of the activities, making mental notes of highlights you perceive and feel during the run-throughs.

Revealing perceptions will automatically come to the fore since your mind is clear and focused in E.F. In this way, as my patients have told me time and time again, the "movie-viewing" will expose vividly *where you can improve and increase the pleasures from your sexual activities*.

Now, while zeroing in on your imaginary screen, ask yourself some of the following questions:

Phase I: "Am I fully sexually stimulated by *desire* . . . and what is it that stirs me up the most?"

Phase II: "Am I intensely sexually *excited?*" Male: "Is my penis fully erect and am I deeply aware and enjoying fully the surging sensation of blood rushing to my genitals?" Female: "Do my genitals feel throbbing and tingling . . . am I fully lubricated and eager for him to enter my vagina?" Both: "Am I totally keyed up, eager for coupling and orgasm?"

Phase III: "Am I fully aware and participating and making the most of the contractions of the genital muscles during orgasm? Am I contributing unreservedly to bringing on an overwhelmingly electrifying orgasm every time? Am I, and my partner, giving each other enough time to rise to maximum excitement so that our orgasms zoom to highest peaks of supreme, extended rapture?"

Phase IV: "Do I and my partner convey to each other our deepest feelings, affection, and tenderness *after* orgasm? Do we extend the period fully for the most satisfaction?"

Considering and examining your answers to these questions and more that may occur to you and your partner can help multiply your total benefits and gratification from sex and love—not just now but through the years. Always take the time for Phase IV!

Augmenting Sexual Pleasure Each Time

Step 2: Once it has become clear to you through E.F. how and in what phases particularly you can improve your sexual enjoyment, you should do the following:

a). Tell and discuss with your partner thoroughly what you have discovered from your awakened understanding. Then communicate your desire to intensify the pleasures of your entire relationship and expanding sexual potential for each of you.

b). Use the E.F. technique time after time, to get the most from any and all of the four phases of sexual intercourse for yourself and your partner. The possibilities for better sex are multiplied if your partner will learn and use the Erotic Focus methodology too.

Applying E.F. Most Effectively in All Phases

To utilize the intensified brain activity in Phase I to its fullest power, concentrate now in retrospect on which action and procedure in sexual intercourse is most exciting and inciting to you. But first, go into E.F. to make the most of your brain processes.

Now check for yourself, recalling which one or more of the following elements elevates your desire to the greatest degree:

Visual stimulation?

Sense of smell?

Touch, feel, caress, massage, rub?

Auditory—certain sounds, specific words, phrases, sentences, music?

Inner mental imagery, fantasies, imagined scenes and actions?

Combination of some or all these elements?

Additional personal arousal factors? (Jot them down to remember and use in the future.)

Let's assume that you personally respond particularly at this time to *visual* stimuli for sexual arousal. Realizing this now, refresh your mind by going into the E.F. state again. Now picture on your mind's E.F. screen various sexual scenes, close-ups of faces, body areas, other pictures that excite you. If you prefer not to project the images on a "screen" in your mind, just let the visuals float about rhythmically in your head while in E.F.

Your personal "brain computer" enables you to recall and project all these images in seconds—just as a mechanical computer comes up with answers to many complex mathematical problems almost instantly.

One visual example of a common *male* fantasy is that the picture on the screen or floating through the mind is of whatever type of woman is most "sexy" to the individual. She may have flaming red hair, be slender and yet voluptuous with long, curvesome legs, a buttock-molding skirt, a tight T-shirt which bulges with her round, full breasts, the nipples taut, elevated and thrusting against the thin fabric . . .

Her face is smoothly exquisite . . . pouting full red lips, a little open and moist . . . her large, sensuous dark eyes looking straight at and into your steaming psyche . . . her total expression eager, inviting, at the boiling-over point . . .

Desire begins building within the man to join with her in sexual play . . . to add the other sensory incitements . . . to touch, to feel, to hold, to caress, to kiss . . . and on to insertion and unrestrained sexual explosion . . .

In a comparable instance of your choice, encouraged and excited increasingly by your E.F. focus, you can indulge yourself in *your* most arousing fantasy. Exert your mental capacities to enjoy most the multitude of available sensations as you utilize fully the Phase I "desire" stage of the sexual response. Let your fantasies build . . . consciously, rapturously . . .

Having become immersed in the sensuous scene, and enjoying Phase I, go on to the following:

1. Remain in E.F., then move into Phase II (excitement) . . . enjoying purposefully and thus fully the inflaming sensations, not holding back . . . climbing to the peak . . .

2. On to Phase III on your inner imaginary screen . . . into orgasm . . . most thrilling, extended, satisfying orgasm . . . hold the sensations, feel them, on and on . . .

3. Here the E.F. state that has alerted you thrillingly will slip away naturally as you prolong fullest sexual intercourse sensations with your partner. The *effects* of your Erotic Focus float in Phase I, though mostly dissipated now, will continue to enhance and extend your functioning and intensity of enjoyment—as you become considerably more aroused than if you had not initiated and entered your E.F. state.

You can employ the easy, abbreviated version of entering the E.F. state throughout all the Phases of intercourse . . . moving out of the Erotic Focus float as you please, or letting it dissipate by itself—no pressure, no compulsion with E.F. Since your senses are heightened in E.F., the entire sexual adventure is felt far more intensively than if you don't use all your senses purposefully.

As you learn how wonderfully the Erotic Focus technique works for you in enhancing your sexual enjoyment and more total fulfillment, you'll wish to teach the simple exercise to your partner. You can impart the technique either fully, step by step, in preparation for sex or the abbreviated form which can be extended throughout intercourse.

6

GAINING SEXUAL CONFIDENCE TO ERASE SEXUAL SHYNESS

Ask yourself, whether you're a woman or a man: "Does my excessive shyness often get in my way to prevent my fullest enjoyment of sex?"

If your answer is yes, then you too are a victim of a very common difficulty which blocks or diminishes the pleasure of better sex for many. That's one of the major laments about sex that I hear in my practice: "Time after time I'm eager to get acquainted with someone who attracts me. Yet I can't bring myself to speak up, to make a move. My problem is that I'm too shy."

There are different shades of meaning to the phrase "being shy." You might be bashful or self-conscious, somewhat retiring or timid. Perhaps you're very distrustful, insecure, modest, even coy. Whatever type of shyness afflicts you, and you'll read more about the kinds of shyness shortly, it adds up to a blockage that gets in the way of your maximum participation and enjoyment of something desirable—because you *hold back*.

Obviously, some shyness can be a good thing, as when it keeps you from possible costly and dangerous excesses such as being overly trusting or promiscuous.

Again, as in so much of living, the goal is *balance*. You want to get the utmost available pleasure from sexual participation. But you don't wish to go overboard to the point of becoming sexually obsessed. Uncontrolled aggressiveness and self-indulgence can be destructive to yourself and your relationship.

You'll learn here further just how the Erotic Focus method can help you achieve the desired *balance*. E.F. can aid you in arriving at insights so you can see and understand a more intelligent course of action. With a reasoned assessment of personal and outside factors, you can better avoid being thwarted by obstructive shyness—without tipping over into risky excessive boldness and harmful pushiness. *You can see more clearly* when you are in the E.F. state.

How to Measure Excessive Shyness

When someone comes to me for help with "a pain," I, or any physician, must try to find out first just where the pain exists, and what causes it. So it's essential that you understand what exactly is meant by excessive "sexual shyness" and the underlying cause of it. Once the source of the restrictive feeling has been tracked down, then remedial treatment—in this instance, self-treatment—can be started and carried through toward a successful conclusion. I have found that sexual shyness can generally be classified in two broad categories:

1. Recognizing *Physical* Shyness

Here again, for clearest understanding, consider which of the following two common sources might most aptly apply to you.

First, some people who at times feel a genuine lack of desire and therefore are unwilling to engage in sexual activities, attribute it to shyness. Actually they may have an innate *low sex drive*. This could be due to genetic causes (inherited, organic), as well as other possible influences such as cultural and family backgrounds. It's a natural built-in fact that different people have different levels of sex drives—high, medium, or low—just as with other physical appetites.

How do you rate yourself here? Consider whether you may have an inherent "low" or "medium" sex drive, for example. If so, you might regard yourself as shy, simply because you haven't a "high" sexual appetite and don't participate in sex as much as reported by others. Realize that many people exaggerate such claims.

Second, if the individual has a conviction that she or he is physically unattractive, that also can be a primary cause of feeling "sexual shyness." Physical attractiveness is often mainly a matter of *inner* perceptions—considering one's self unlovely or homely or ugly usually stems not from actual unattractiveness but from how an individual sees herself (or himself) in the mind's eye. Much of the time, such people put themselves down because they think incorrectly that their bodies are negatively "different," even "deformed" in ways that turn others off. A woman may feel that her breasts are too large or too small, one larger or smaller than the other in a "freakish" way. She might be overly sensitive about a thick growth of hair in the pubic area, a few hairs growing between the breasts or elsewhere, a birthmark on the torso, veiny thighs, and so on. She labels herself falsely as "unattractive."

I've learned from men who complain of being sexually

shy that the trigger often is concern about what they regard as diminutive penis size. Other men consider themselves unattractive due to having too much hair or little hair growth on the body, or having only one testicle (undescended due to an abnormality at birth). Other evidences, usually insignificant, may create a false or distorted self-image leading to emotional overkill.

Sexual shyness may be brought on, often with the person not being really conscious of the reason, as a result of surgery or injuries. Even minor scars resulting from an appendectomy, breast surgery, hysterectomy, other operations leave some supersensitive individuals feeling extremely unattractive.

Yet many people hide from themselves the fact that they feel unsightly and instead insist, "I'm just naturally too shy to have sex . . ." Think about it, please: Have you some real or imagined "defect" which has been magnified in your mind, making you "sexually shy?" Facing the truth can help to set you free from your restrictive shyness, as you'll learn in case histories that follow shortly.

2. Recognizing *Psychological* Shyness

Sexual shyness is far more often due to psychological factors than sound physical reasons. The most prevalent causes of sexual inhibitions are listed here. Checking them carefully and then following through constructively on any that may apply to you can be a mind-opener and a lifelong sexual advantage for you.

CHECKLIST OF PSYCHOLOGICAL INFLUENCES

"**Sex is dirty.**" *Distorted moral values* imbued during childhood make many shy away from sexual contact.

The confused adolescent and adult must act to overcome the negative attitude that sex is dirty, then approach sex as a normal activity that can be beautifully rewarding, as explained throughout these pages.

"**Good girls don't do this.**" *Twisted cultural standards* can instill a feeling in a woman that sexual desire and participation brands her as a tramp and a man as a pervert. Clear self-analysis in Erotic Focus can free one from such misconceptions.

"**Sex is a sin.**" *Strict religious rules* or *distorted religious concepts* inhibit some individuals throughout life from reaching out sexually. Sound knowledge about sexuality and love can help the person to clear understanding.

"**He's below my class.**" "**She's above me.**" *Deep-seated class consciousness,* social and/or economic, keeps some from sexual contacts: "She's too rich; she'll think I'm after her money." Or, "I mustn't lower myself, he's the pits." False standards, unless straightened out, can inhibit fullest sexual enjoyment lifelong.

"**I'm inept, I'll foul things up.**" *Lack of sexual knowledge* makes many avoid sexual contact, because of anxiety, fear of failure and rejection. What you'll learn in this book, and sharpen with your E.F. technique, can transform ignorance into eagerness and success.

"**My looks will turn him/her off.**" *A poor physical self-image* tends not only to turn others away but also to turn off sexual openness by the self-derogating woman or man. A frank, clear look at oneself on the Erotic Focus inner mirror can boost self-confidence and chase sexual timidity.

"**I can't speak up, I get tongue-tied.**" *Lack of com-*

munication skills restrains many from sexual approaches. Learning how to communicate (Chapter 4), and planning ahead through E.F. sharpened perception, can help you reach out instead of pulling away.

"I messed up in my first affair, I'll fail again." *Fear of failure* after one or more bad sexual experiences may cause a person to repress sexual desires and pleasures for life. Examining all facets of a defeat objectively through the revealing Erotic Focus method can switch destructive looking back to optimistic moving forward.

Understanding and Handling Sexual Shyness

Once you have realized that one or more of the listed factors contribute to any burdensome sexual shyness that may be thwarting you, what can you do to correct the situation? The remedial steps are not difficult. It has been my gratifying experience that most individuals who are affected negatively by sexual shyness can overcome the problem quite easily.

Basically, it's very encouraging that a certain degree of sexual shyness is entirely within the range of normal human behavior. Therefore it becomes important not to exaggerate such reticent behavior in your mind. I see this unwarranted, destructive overemphasis occurring often among younger people especially, women and men who are in the early stages of their sexual adventuring. Due to uncertainty, anxiety, inexperience, and other natural elements in the checklist, they feel insecure and shy.

Also, to a smaller degree, the problems can recur—and repeatedly—in persons who are not sexually shy in general, but somewhat apprehensive when starting a relationship with a new partner, and then being together sexually for the first time or the first few encounters. Undoubtedly this has happened to you, and you probably felt timid and unstrung.

This kind of shyness is generally self-limiting; it usually dissipates as soon as the partners know each other better and their continuing relationship develops a feeling of mutual ease and possibly increasing fervor. A real problem arises only if timidity and even fearfulness persists in a continuing association. In the latter case, you'll probably do well to regard the ''shyness'' as a possible warning signal from your unconscious to reassess the linkage carefully. It may also indicate that you have other deeper problems, and perhaps you should seek some outside help at this point.

It's valuable to know that a person who may experience some social insecurity and be shy in social settings is not necessarily sexually shy as well. Although, as in most situations, a variety of factors may be involved, I can assure you that a number of my patients who complained of severe insecurities in other areas were functioning very well sexually. The opposite is true also, of course. Just don't take it for granted that the socially adept person you meet is the same sexually (note, for example, Gail's case history later in this chapter).

Effective Two-Step Method to Control Excessive Shyness

Please study the following simple step-by-step Erotic Focus self-treatment procedure and learn it well. You'll find that you can apply the same kind of "self-programming" to practically any type of sexual relationship problem or concern you have or may develop at some time. The technique will improve your approach and functioning for better sex in general.

Step 1: Sight Your Personal Problem Clearly

Go into the E.F. state in privacy, as you have already learned.

In the E.F. float, using the TV-screen technique, project on the screen a scene of a situation based on the prime psychological factor (or more than one, successively) that fits you personally, as you identified in the checklist.

For example, if your primary problem is "lack of communication skills," replay on your mind's screen in E.F. a typical situation where you met someone you liked but were tongue-tied. Now visualize yourself saying something interesting, clever, humorous, and thus communicating easily and well. Practice in your E.F. state all the things you might say, again and again . . .

If none of the listed problems quite fits you, then allow your mind free rein (while in E.F., of course, relaxed and yet mentally very alert) to spur your thoughts and anxieties about sex to surface inside you and project clearly upon the screen . . .

Whatever your particular concerns which make you sexually shy, replay a series of situations from the past where the hang-ups occurred or where they might take place now. Focus on the specific scenes and details of your embarrassment and withdrawal mentally and/or physically . . .

Now you are concentrating on the dilemmas, not running away. You're taking an all-important step to examine and get rid of your sexual shyness by facing the reality and then sighting the solution at hand.

Step 2: Design Your Stage-by-Stage Solution

Now that you have a clear idea of what feelings, situations and concerns trigger your shyness, let's move ahead to design your personal program to overcome the blockage and be free of this hang-up.

For instance, if your sexual shyness is due to the fear of being rejected by your proposed partner, ask yourself probing questions, while your mind is especially alive and most creative in your E.F. float. Query yourself along lines such as:

"What does this relationship, now or in the future, really mean to me? How important is it to me?"

"How much do I value my partner, and how does this affect or add to or diminish how I value myself?"

"If I am rejected, can I handle it calmly, or would it damage me for a long time, perhaps irreparably?"

Obviously these are serious questions which you should ask and answer for yourself. Confronting and answering them while in your freer and more enlightened state of Erotic Focus can lead you to startling and liberating revelations. For example, if you find that a turndown wouldn't be totally devastating, then you might realize, "So what if he rejects me? It's not that big a deal," and your shyness lessens, along with your fear of failure.

Bolstered by your realistic "So what?" attitude, you take a chance. You make the approach. If the reaction is welcoming, you go on openly from there. If you get a cold reception, "So what?—I'll seek further opportunities elsewhere. Sooner or later I'll come up with a winner."

As another example, suppose your shyness is based on inability to speak up. You're in a relationship which isn't fully satisfying, yet you're too "shy" to voice your discontent, to try to make things right for both of you. What to do? Go into the E.F. float, pinpoint visually exactly what is troubling you most. That realization will help you bring the main irritant out in the open. If you see clearly that you really care about him or her enough to continue the relationship, you'll have to work on the problem together.

If the answer to yourself is that you really don't love the other party enough, then your course is obvious: break it up now before your unhappiness deepens. On the other hand, if you find that you both are very important to each other, then it becomes easier to communicate your fears without anger or hurtful confrontation.

You might say something like, "I care for you very much, and I know that you feel the same way about me. I'm thrilled when we make love. But . . . there's one special point that's upsetting me, and I'm sure you're not aware of this particular matter. Often lately you start talking about your previous girlfriend, how gorgeous and how sexy she was. That makes me self-conscious. I become withdrawn and shy because I start doubting whether I can live up to your expectations . . .''

Such open communication can lead to everything becoming better than ever before, fostering an increasing depth of feeling between you—if the relationship is basically solid and sound. If it isn't—again, it's better that you find out now.

If results from talking frankly are unsatisfactory, I suggest that you consider all sides of the matter in E.F. clarity repeatedly over a period of days or longer. You'll sight your best course of action, and move ahead for greater personal contentment one way or the other. You'll discern how to make matters better between you . . . or you'll break it off cleanly.

You can tackle other of the listed possible problems, or any more you may have added, along the same lines. If, after trying the suggested approaches, you still feel overwhelmed by sexual shyness, you might consider professional therapy. If you have a trusting relationship with your physician, or with any other valued counselors, consider seeking their advice about getting further professional help. See Chapter 14 regarding choosing a therapist, if you decide that's desirable in your case.

Before helping you with a few illustrative case histories, it's worth reviewing—for your action now and throughout the future—the two vital steps to help overcome sexual shyness. You can apply this practicable twofold procedure to help remove other prevalent concerns that may get in the way of deriving your fullest possible pleasures from sex:

Step 1: *Sight Your Personal Problem Clearly*
Step 2: *Design Your Stage-by-Stage Solution, and then Follow Through Accordingly*

Giving the Right Signals

Gail, an executive assistant in her midtwenties, sat in my office silently for a moment, displaying obvious reluctance. Finally she said, hesitantly, "I've had a number of unhappy and worrisome experiences with men. I'm pretty sure I was at fault, and I want to investigate where I went wrong . . ."

As she stopped, searching for words, I noted again that she was attractive and appealing, lovely in face and figure. I asked encouragingly, "Where do you think you go 'wrong'?"

"Well," her expression was candid, "I have no trouble meeting men. They seem to like me. I'm friendly and, I guess, inviting. We get along well at first . . ." Again she paused, seemed somewhat embarrassed.

"What happens then?"

She laughed nervously, "Then things get fouled up. We enjoy each other's company, reveal a lot, laugh a lot. But when it comes to having sex after some enjoyable dates, I become very self-conscious and fearful. Even though I want sex, I find myself pushing the man away. I don't know why . . . I just feel terribly shy . . ."

"How far do you go before you back away?"

"Oh . . ." she proceeded slowly, "past kissing and all that—right up to when we're in bed together naked—then suddenly I get nervous or scared or something. I untangle myself, get up, get dressed, and end the evening right there. I say I feel sick or queasy . . . or some other dumb excuse . . ."

"Does that end the relationship?"

She seemed angry, "Sometimes they never even call back to find out how I am." She finished disgustedly, "Then I know I was right, that I just can't trust any man . . . isn't that true?"

As we talked on, it became clear to me that she attracted men with her physical beauty and seductive air. For instance, she wore sexy clothes—obviously she could arouse a man easily. However, she didn't realize that she was being physically and verbally enticing. She emphasized, "I'm not interested in just a physical relationship—I want an intellectual and deeply emotional attachment."

I pointed out that she wasn't wrong to expect intellectual and emotional caring as part of a sexual involvement. I asked, "Did you ever consider whether you may have been unintentionally giving out the *wrong signals* to the men you meet whom you like?"

I encouraged Gail (as you learned earlier) to visualize a TV screen in her mind while in her Erotic Focus float. On the screen she was to project "movies" of her last few unsuccessful encounters with men, examining every detail of what went on from the start of her meeting the man—and the very upsetting windup.

She told me later that, watching her moves clearly in the E.F. reenactment, she was shocked. For the first time she realized quickly that right from the beginning—in her revealing low-cut blouse and split skirt, in her beckoning "body language," in her behavior of touching and clinging—she came across as a tease and a pushover from the first date onward.

For example, she understood by examining the E.F. replay that after some kissing and petting—in the taxi or car or elsewhere—it seems a come-on to the man when you accept an invitation to go up to his apartment, and then have a few stiff drinks. Gail commented with an air of discovery, "I know that such actions, especially these days, imply that you're ready and eager to jump into bed. I guess that's okay when you want it, but in my case, my natural shyness interfered, and I overreacted badly—"

"You appeared ready, but you really weren't," I suggested, "because of your reticence in not wanting to violate your own high standards. You didn't want sex without caring, love, respect."

"Yes," she admitted, freed by her new comprehension. "It wasn't the man's fault. I shouldn't have gone to his apartment, but should have put that off until I came to know him better. I should have suggested coffee or a drink in some neutral place like a restaurant."

I agreed, "You definitely were giving out the wrong signals, considering that you value your self-respect highly. Toward the end of the evening, if you liked him, you might have told him honestly that you enjoyed his company but that you weren't ready for sex until you both knew each other better."

It all worked out extremely well for Gail—as the two-step E.F. system probably can for you if you proceed thoughtfully and patiently to apply it properly. Gail *sighted her personal problem,* that she dressed and acted contrary to her true character. Then she *designed her solution*—to moderate her appearance and conduct, and then to be honest and aboveboard with others, men and women, and with herself.

By understanding the true reasons for her "sexual shyness," and communicating openly with the men she dated, Gail explained to me happily some time later, "I felt released from timidity and fear. I could be myself. I have a wonderful relationship now with a man whom I had rejected angrily before. He phoned me again, said he wanted to understand. We met and talked things through. He has become a super companion and lover."

Transforming "Loser" into "Winner"

Sidney arrived in my office, shy and embarrassed. I noted that he was a pleasant-looking man in his early thirties, a bit shorter than average but not exceptionally so. He was wearing a nondescript dark grey suit, and his entire bearing reflected a lack of self-confidence.

He had difficulty looking me in the eye, and he spoke softly in a monotone. It developed that he had "a good job" as a computer operator in a large company. He consulted me because he realized that his overpowering shyness was keeping him from advancing at work and primarily that his relations with women were poor due to his being also excessively shy socially and sexually.

As he opened up, he explained, "I want to meet a nice woman, get married and have kids. Yet, whenever

I'm with someone who attracts me, I clam up. I've had some dates, after pushing myself hard, but when the situation develops to the point of really making love, I get confused and embarrassed by my shyness. I back off, and usually leave right away."

He said that he was physically sexually capable. "But I have sex only with prostitutes. I treat that as a commercial proposition, so I get my orgasms but no real satisfaction." He mumbled, "When it comes to 'nice girls,' I realize that I'm not much to look at . . . I haven't a dynamite personality or the gift of gab. I can't hand out a line that breaks the ice quickly . . . I'm pretty much a washout."

As we talked he began to understand that he was frustrated by a very negative self-image, that he underrated himself and had a false picture of his appearance, personality and appeal. As he practiced and learned the Erotic Focus method, he began to find some needed relief from the tensions and insecurities he had imposed upon himself. He started to accept himself as a functioning individual rather than as "a loser," as he put it.

In Step 1, *sighting his personal problem clearly,* in the E.F. float he re-created in his mind his encounters with women as they actually happened—not as distorted by his own downgrading self-portrait. He could see—in the freedom and clarity of E.F. revelation—that women found his appearance acceptable, that they regarded him and his comments pleasantly, even indicated a liking for him.

I suggested as the next stage that he visualize himself on the E.F. screen in new meetings with women, imagining what he would *like* to happen sexually and otherwise. He could fantasize on scenes of loving sex in which he and his partner participated fully, not holding back, not being sidetracked by shyness.

Gradually he came to see himself as he was truly—if not a "ball of fire," at least as an attractive, personable, desirable man. With this revised, upgraded and more accurate self-image, his social and other activities improved markedly, and Sidney was definitely on his way to a less inhibited, happier life. I suggested that he continue his Erotic Focus exercises daily. This was not only desirable, but often a necessity, for a constant renewal and refreshing of his clear insights. Also he'd be bolstering his self-confidence, as insurance to keep the oppression of excessive sexual shyness from returning.

Fine-Tuning an Out-of-Focus Body Image

Clara is an example of the fact that sexual shyness can interfere with a person's maximum enjoyment of life at just about any age and situation. When I first saw her she was in her late forties, with two grown children and, as she stated with some wonderment, "A fine husband who still loves me in spite of the mess I've become."

In addition to the problem she explained of relatively recent sexual shyness, she said that she felt "generally depressed about practically everything. There's little in life that I've really enjoyed during the past year. I can't see any happiness in my future." She had called me at the suggestion of her surgeon who had done a partial mastectomy on one breast, with radiation follow-up as part of her cancer therapy.

Clara went through the surgery very well, was healing desirably, but found it very difficult to accept what had happened to her. Now she burst out as she faced me, "I feel victimized! Maybe it sounds ridiculous to others, but I'm damned angry at my body for having developed cancer. All my adult life I've been careful about my eating, I've been active and have exercised regularly—then *boom,* my body turns on me. *Why me?*"

Lest you think that this case is unusual and extreme, and may not have any application to you, be reassured that you can learn from Clara's problem and self-treatment. I've seen women and men afflicting themselves similarly over small or sizable blemishes, wrinkling, overweight, being "too short" or "too tall" or "too homely"—and any number of minor or major difficulties. These expressed "shortcomings" may be actual or imagined conditions which, in their cases, triggered sexual shyness.

When I questioned Clara about her sex life, she reacted by breaking out in tears and sobbing. "That's the great tragedy," she cried. "My husband and I used to have sex often—and we both enjoyed it thoroughly—until shortly before my surgery. Now I can't even undress before him, I've become so painfully shy. I'm worse than an inhibited schoolgirl. When Jack reaches to touch me, I back away instantly. I want him but I'm so ashamed of my body, I'm fearful of being rejected."

"Does your husband seem reluctant to kiss and hug and fondle you?"

"No, quite the opposite," she protested. "He says that I'm beautiful to him, that he loves me more than ever, that he wants to be close to me. He's badly hurt when I cringe away. But you understand why I've become so skittish. I feel that my body has been mutilated, that I'm ugly and repellent. I was always proud of my firm breasts, but now—'' She added anxiously, ''As a woman, you must agree . . .''

I certainly did *not* agree, neither as a woman nor as a psychiatrist. I cite this case particularly because it encompasses a number of causes for sexual shyness embodied in the checklist: ''Fear of rejection . . . irrational anxieties . . . low self-esteem . . . poor body image . . . personal insecurity . . . false self-perception.'' Please read my following instructions to Clara slowly and carefully in order to learn and apply them yourself if you are at all afflicted with sexual shyness.

Stage 1: I taught Clara the Erotic Focus method, which she learned very quickly. She reported that she was starting to get some soothing relief from the overpowering self-pressure. Then I instructed her as follows:

''While in E.F., concentrate your mind on this— which is the *truth* about your condition: Even though your body admittedly has changed, you are *alive.* Let that sink in, please—you are *alive* . . .

''Now, rather than seeing yourself as a 'victim,' look at your body as an *instrument for living.* Your body has been put through serious illness, but has *made it!* Rather than hating your body, learn to love it and protect it as much as possible . . .

''Also—so important—give your body pleasure, *physical pleasure.* There is more to you than just a breast. *Enjoy the rest of your body*—starting right now, and continuing. Concentrate on that, on giving your body and yourself pleasure from now on.''

Have you digested that suggestion? It may refer to you too if you have a poor body image. Focus on the positive while in E.F.—and get the clear-sighted lift that will come with repeated concentration and understanding.

Stage 2: I told Clara, ''With the aid of E.F. comprehension, examine your body in the mirror; get acquainted with your 'new self.' Touch yourself here and there and all over. Realize and enjoy deeply the fact that your body is alive, functioning, feeling . . .

''Now—this is very important—make friends particularly with any parts of your body that may have changed. Get to know yourself better and appreciate what you *have*.''

Stage 3: ''Tell your husband [partner, lover, friend] openly how you feel about yourself and your body— and that you have learned how to accept it and make the most of it as it is. Now show your body clearly to him—don't hide in the dark and under covers. Show him your 'new' body—with pride in your new understanding which gives you both a new lease on life. Instead of rejecting contact, encourage him to touch the skin on your breast, and to caress you lovingly and excitedly all over.''

To Clara's surprise and delight, her husband was *not* terrified or turned off by looking at the scar and burn marks. He very quickly was touching her lovingly and pleasurably everywhere—without feeling any of the aversion and reluctance she had anticipated and feared. She found that, as she had learned for herself, he was overwhelmingly happy that she was *alive,* that he could now receive her full love again, and give his own freely.

Step by step, they resumed their sex life, as in the past. Her depression lifted and she stopped coming for therapy. In saying goodbye she told me, "I don't experience any sexual shyness at all anymore. Our enjoyment of sex and our love have deepened through this shared experience. E.F. was a great help in lifting me from my fog of confusion. It enabled me to see and understand the possibilities clearly."

From Shying Away . . . to Full Sexual Intercourse

There are variations of "shyness" which may manifest themselves in differing ways. Many people, probably you at times, feel "inadequate" sexually for one reason or another, and *you cannot admit your true feelings even to yourself.* This can result in shying away from full sexual activity and maximum sexual enjoyment, without really knowing why.

Bill, a lawyer in his late twenties, came to see me because he had never permitted himself full sexual intercourse with a woman. He wanted desperately to change that. An attractive, well-groomed man, very successful in his career, he had dated many women over the years. He said that he was basically very shy, and tried to cover that up by trying to appear dynamic and even aggressive.

Sexually he had gone as far as intensive petting and manipulation, and had become "expert" (as he stated) at bringing women to orgasm. But he had never allowed full penis insertion and intercourse to occur. He usually brought himself to orgasm alone later by masturbating.

He explained to me that he was too embarrassed by what he considered his small, inadequate penis to uncover and insert it—in spite of getting an erection readily. *He couldn't accept the truth, in spite of assurance from his doctor, that the small size of his penis was not a barrier to full sexual performance.* Now he'd become involved with a woman he loved very much. They were making plans to get married and start a family in the near future. She was putting pressure on him to have sexual intercourse.

He realized that he couldn't pretend any longer. Nor would it be fair for him to even consider marriage as long as he felt inadequate and shunned penis exposure. He admitted that he felt crushed by his dilemma, couldn't think straight, that there was no solution in sight: *"What can I do?"* he asked desperately.

I explained that he was obsessed by a false notion, shared by many others. Some men were embarrassed or ashamed by the conviction that they were too hairy, too short, too uneducated, unintelligent. Some women denied themselves full sexual enjoyment because they thought their breasts were too tiny or too huge or deformed in one way or another. Many women suffered from feeling too fat or too thin, ashamed of having too heavy thighs or veiny legs or any number of other self-imposed "flaws" or inadequacies.

I explained to Bill that in order to help himself view and analyze his situation accurately, the Erotic Focus technique could be a great aid. First, he had to realize that sex is just one part, although an important one, in a loving relationship. Vaginal intercourse and orgasm are desirable contributors but only segments rather than the whole of love between partners.

So far as his so-called penis deficiency went, he was ahead of many other men in that he'd become "expert," in his own words, in vital aspects of sex such as caressing, kissing, oral sex, masturbation of a partner, to bring her to top excitement and orgasm. Thus he had a big advantage over the many men who concentrated mainly on "getting there" themselves, and "scoring." Women justifiably hate to be left unsatisfied or considered just another "score."

I suggested to Bill that he measure his penis during erection. He reported, "Five inches." He was amazed to hear that the statistical range of measure of the average male penis when erect was four to eight inches; therefore his penis was "normal."

Also, it was pointed out that he should know from personal experience that caressing and expert manipulation were most desirable in leading a woman to orgasm, that female sensitivity was greatest at the entrance *(introitus)* of the vagina rather than in the depth of the vagina itself .. *so the length of the penis is relatively unimportant for fullest sexual pleasure.*

I taught Bill the Erotic Focus method and told him to do it at least five to ten times daily. While in E.F., he was to visualize himself in the nude, realizing that his penis size was normal, that the blockage was in his mind and not a physical inadequacy.

He was also to proceed to intercourse with his fiancee, as she wanted. He should not reveal any past concern about penis size, but should undress with her in the light, or dark, whatever he felt comfortable with.

Then, in bed he should encourage her to fondle and kiss his penis while he touched and caressed her all over, proceeding to insertion, full intercourse, and mutual orgasm.

He was to go into E.F. before intercourse, informing her about it or not, as he wished. He could refresh his E.F. state in seconds at any time if he found himself becoming at all tense and anxious. Since the exercise took only seconds each time, and could be done in the concealed "quickie" manner if more fitting, it would work smoothly to control and dissipate any fears.

In a few weeks he had lost his penis concerns completely and had reached his goal of total sexual intercourse. He told me laughingly in parting, "What a fool I've been all these years. I missed so many opportunities for sexual fulfillment!"

"Let me rephrase that," I interjected. "Rather than considering yourself a fool, look at it this way: You perfected your skills at lovemaking to please a woman. Now that you've found the right, enduring partner, you took the last step—and you're over your feeling of inadequacy and so-called shyness. Congratulations—enjoy!"

7

HOW TO ENJOY SEXUAL FANTASIES FOR BETTER SEX

You've probably heard and read a lot about sexual fantasies, pro and con, and you may be a little confused about the subject. I'd like to clarify for you how sexual fantasizing, in necessary moderation, can help you gain maximum sexual pleasure and rewards. Basically, it's my professional experience that (paraphrasing a wise comment in another area) *most negative criticism of sexual fantasizing is not about the use of a bad thing but the abuse of a good thing.*

Sexual fantasies, applied well, sensibly, without excess, can bring you increased enjoyment of sex. If such fantasies are exaggerated, and carried through excessively, so that the unreal replaces the real completely, then serious consequences can result, as in the following case history.

Some time back, Jessica came to see me. She was the divorced mother of a grown daughter who had insisted that her mother visit me. "My daughter is wrong," Jessica insisted angrily, "but I agreed to humor her by consulting you. The fact is that I've fallen in love with a famous English rock star, Shelley. At first I just dreamed about him again and again. But my love has grown more and more. Now I'm convinced that he's in love with me too.''

Before I could respond, she added emphatically, "I *know* it. There's no question about it.''

Jessica's daughter had informed me that her mother had become so obsessed with Shelley that she had sold most of her possessions. Despite all protests, she had used the money to travel to London. She had tracked down the star, but his associates had refused to let her see him.

"Everybody around Shelley is jealous," she insisted. "I know he's crazy about me, wants to make love to me, just as I want him. But the authorities forced me to get on a plane. They made me return here. Everybody, including my daughter, is keeping us apart. It's a plot against us. Can you help me reach him and see him instead of my just dreaming about him?''

Clearly this is a case where Jessica's personal problems in other areas took her far past a normal level of sexual fantasizing. She had to be admitted to the hospital for extended treatment to help her let go of her totally unrealistic fantasies. The cause of the trouble was not the sexual fantasizing itself, but deeply rooted and complex difficulties that had long beset her. Nevertheless, this case illustrates the importance of not going overboard in fantasizing, as in anything else.

How Fantasy Can Be Helpful

Psychologically, fantasy can provide an outlet to relieve and satisfy, if only temporarily but still effectively, a person's sexual wishes and drives. Consider the fact that a multimillion-dollar business—the publishing of romance books—is built almost totally on romantic sexual fantasies, daydreaming, imagining, transference—call it what you will. These books cater to hidden wishes and desires of many women by having the fantasies actualized on paper.

Many males find similar substitution and some release in the pages of magazines such as *Playboy, Penthouse*, and many other publications. They cater fundamentally to the "visual arousal mechanism" in men, and to some degree in women through comparable publications. Lush photographs and drawings trigger the reader's fantasies about the models pictured, providing imaginative surrogate involvement and sexual excitement.

Every human being possesses a wide range of sexual activities *confined to the mind alone*. This includes fleeting sexual images, detailed fantasies, fading sexual memories, projected hopes and expectations. There should never be any guilt attached to this. There are few, if any, humans who do not have some sexual fantasies. Many people spend a good deal of time each day in sexual fantasy while doing something else—driving a car, doing routine work, listening to tiresome talk. Masturbation also is accompanied usually by vivid imagery. It may be a relief for you to know that this is quite common practice, not perverted, depraved, or "immoral."

Consider what practically everyone has experienced—that a person in love spends a great deal of time daydreaming and fantasizing about the object of the overwhelming affection. In the private and safe realm of the mind, one can rehearse and replay favorite fantasies endlessly—sometimes in a continuing and expanding series, with titillating variations of the same theme. Fantasizing provides pleasure for the individual, and no harm to anyone else.

Benefits of Sexual Fantasizing

When the subject of sexual fantasies comes up in conversation, too many people have the knee-jerk reaction that fantasizing is "good" or it's "bad." For you, the individual, the point is not a general "good" or "bad," but what *you* are comfortable with. What fantasies can increase your sexual pleasure? What fantasies violate your principles and feelings, and therefore should be restricted in your mind for *yourself?*

Only you can answer those questions honestly and precisely. But, happily, the Erotic Focus method you've learned, practiced, and now use will help you reach top rewards from fantasizing.

The personally selected fantasies, especially enjoyed during your E.F. float, aid you in rehearsing your future best sexual functioning, and in choreographing your behavior patterns in advance. You will see more clearly if you have any disruptive patterns of anxiety, guilt, excessive shyness and withdrawal.

Furthermore, as you participate in the fantasies, your mental computer acts to *reprogram* your feelings and actions for a more productive and enriching sexual life. If, for example, you are in a state of some boredom and unfulfilling routine in your sexual life, fantasizing can provide what I call *creative enrichment*. This simply means that you will be able to devise new solutions that work for you, just as they proved effective in the following case history . . .

New Life for a Sexually Bored Couple

Diana, a fashion designer in her late twenties, was referred to me for treatment of a mild depression. She said that she had married Warren, a lawyer just a little older, five years before. She described their overall relationship as "happy and satisfactory."

While taking her sexual history as she started therapy, it became obvious that there was some sexual maladjustment involved. I asked along the way, "How often do you and your husband have sexual intercourse generally?"

"Two or three times a week, quite regularly. . ."

"And, as you said," I commented, "it's 'happy and satisfactory' . . ."

She was silent, then spoke slowly. "Well . . . I don't really enjoy sexual intercourse much any more. . . . I rarely have an orgasm. Oh, I come once in a while, but usually—nothing."

As therapy continued, it became clear that Diana

was disturbed considerably by the fact that she was having fantasies based on a recurring *homosexual* theme.

"While Warren is pumping away at me in our bed," she said, "I often see in my mind a strange woman sitting in the room with us. She is leaning forward toward us in the large armchair facing the bed. She's naked, except for a wide pleated skirt. Her legs are apart so that her crotch is open, exposed and moist. Crouching toward us, her big breasts sway loosely—as her gaze is riveted on us . . ."

Staring straight ahead, Diane continued, clearly agitated, "I become very excited as the woman begins stroking her clitoris, and caresses herself. Then she gets up, comes over. She joins in our lovemaking, rubs herself against Warren as she fondles my breasts and my genitals. Soon she lowers her head, her hair spreading over me as she begins sucking and kissing my clitoris urgently . . ." She stopped, her face flaming, her eyes dazed, reliving the imaginary scene.

I asked whether this fantasy brought her to climax.

"Sometimes . . ." She frowned, thinking. "Mostly I feel guilty and try to block the image out of my head— and that turns me off sex completely. Sometimes I don't even try. I just go through the motions until Warren comes—and it's over. But when he's inside me and I let the fantasy lady have her way, licking and sucking me, my excitement mounts incredibly and I have a fantastic orgasm . . ." Her gaze was fixed at the floor as she became silent.

"Does the orgasm give you release, make you feel good?"

She shook her head dejectedly. "No, I feel overwhelmed by a suffocating sense of guilt, like I'm 'cheat-

ing' on my husband with this woman, this stranger—"
She choked back a sob, then went on, "Also . . . I
worry that I may be a lesbian at heart. That frightens
me most of all."

Upon questioning, she elaborated, "When I was a
teenager, an older female cousin I admired visited us
and stayed over a few times during each year. We
played 'nurse and patient,' with her massaging me and
taking my temperature with a thermometer in my vagina and rectum. Then we would masturbate together.
The next time we would reverse roles, and masturbate
again."

I waited, she went on. "I enjoyed these sex games so
much and I looked forward to her visits. After she
stopped visiting a few years later, I would re-create the
scenes in my mind, and I continued masturbating until
I came—by bringing back in every detail the experiences with my cousin. And," she added in despair, "I
made up similar fantasies of sex play with other
women, strangers to me . . ."

Clasping her hands tightly, visibly upset, she blurted
out, "I'm so frightened and ashamed and guilty and
depressed. I don't know who I am!"

Please read the step-by-step treatment I gave Diana
and consider the possibilities for your own greater sexual ease and enjoyment.

Step 1: Assess the Fantasy Sensibly and Clearly

As Diana and I talked, I was able to help her clarify
and realize for herself that her fantasy was harmless. I
told her (as I assure you) that many people have homo-

sexual fantasies, and that this didn't mean that she was a lesbian. She came to understand that her early masturbatory experiences had *conditioned* her to be turned on sexually by fantasies involving women. But, significantly, over all the ensuing years, she had never formed or even desired a sexual relationship with a woman rather than a man. Those *facts* convinced and reassured her.

Step 2: Use "Better Sex" Fantasies in E.F.

After she had learned and was enjoying using the Erotic Focus method, I suggested to Diana that she might project on the "TV screen" in her mind some new, different sexual fantasies which would reprogram her personal internal arousal mechanism. I recommended that she visualize on the screen fantasies involving her *husband*.

I advised specifically that she should focus on those attributes Warren possessed, especially physical features and characteristics, that she liked most about him. Following up on this thought, she told me later that she loved his thick, luxuriant, dark hair particularly. She created fantasies on the screen in her mind of curling up on a bed with him, naked bodies pressing against each other, her fingers playing erotically with his hair. She said that she became aroused increasingly by feeling the texture, smell, and touch of his hair, and twining the strands between her eager fingers—in her imagination.

Another fantasy she dreamed up was built around the projection on her mental screen of Warren having sex with another woman—energetically, inventively, passionately—in increasing crescendo, right through to heaving, screaming, simultaneous orgasms. Diana explained that in real life she was extremely jealous of her husband, but somehow "seeing" him in roaring sexual exultation with another woman in her fantasy aroused her and made her "horny" to couple with him just as the imaginary female had done.

I suggested that she might enjoy fantasizing about her husband having sex with another woman while she was actually having intercourse with him herself. There was no harm at all in visualizing that while she herself was in his arms. She said that when she tried this, after she went into the E.F. float, she became extraordinarily aroused as he fondled and then thrust his penis into her. She had responded with her body plunging and writhing as never before—until they both came to gasping, overwhelming climax. Smiling at the memory, she said they had remained for what "seemed like hours" in shuddering, loving embrace.

Step 3: Share Fantasies with a Partner

After these reported successes, I suggested to Diana (as I do in many other cases) that she think about communicating some of her sexual fantasies to her husband—for even deeper, mutually shared experiences. However, I cautioned her to mull over carefully beforehand whether it might be better to preserve her privacy, every individual's right, about her lesbian fantasies. Relating these episodes might trouble Warren unnecessarily. Yet she could retain that as her personal privilege for extra sexual pleasure on her own, when desired or needed.

Furthermore, I encouraged Diana to discuss the general subject of fantasies with her husband and find out what his own were or might be. This could help them both to learn and share information and understanding about *his* hidden sexual desires and anxieties, along with hers. This mutual sharing would lead them to continuing and even greater sexual enjoyment. Sure enough, a few weeks later Diana reported that her sexual life, and her husband's, too, had become far more exciting and satisfying. They gained much increased pleasure from sharing mutual sexual fantasies (as well as their private ones). As an extension of fantasizing, they had great additional fun playing sex games (see the next chapter)—all part of creative sexual enrichment.

Reliving Joyous Sexual Memories

Fantasizing can also help you relive happy, warming sexual memories to augment your pleasure in daily living. You can re-create the high points of your past and even build on the actuality to enhance those memorable fulfillments. There can be much sustenance in expanding on the blissful emotions of enriching days and nights you have experienced through the years gone by.

On one level, you may enjoy better sex—by reliving through fantasy on your mind's E.F. screen during intercourse—some especially arousing adventures with other lovers. As long as you keep the fantasizing within bounds—untinged by regret or envy or remorse—you can mine and extract from the past certain pleasing recollections to improve your present and future sex life.

Fantasizing from the past can also, on a deeper level, provide comfort, relief, and at least temporary liberation from pressing problems and oppressive troubles. An example is this case which brought immense personal gratification for me, as well as for my patients . . .

Renewed Happiness in Remembering

A slow-moving gentleman, obviously in pain, was helped into my office by his wife. She introduced herself as Naomi. He, Douglas, had been referred to me by his physician to learn my E.F. technique for reducing his suffering.

He appeared much older, but it turned out that Douglas was just past fifty. He was afflicted with metastatic cancer (inoperable, terminal). He said that he had come to terms with his condition, but desperately sought further relief from his pain, only partially alleviated by large amounts of medication.

It became clear that Naomi was extremely involved and supportive throughout their marriage and now in his suffering. She remained at his side and participated throughout his visits. I taught them both how to enter the E.F. state in order to bring relief from mental and emotional as well as physical torment. I taught Douglas to concentrate during his periods in E.F. on floating lightly and pleasantly, as on a soft cloud, until he was wafted along airily, and his pain reduced in intensity.

During our follow-up sessions, I emphasized that he

was to repeat this type of E.F. float every couple of hours for extended periods. I suggested that Naomi go into the relaxing, relieving E.F. float too, and in the same room with him—if they both wished. They reported that they were obtaining wonderful relief, he from the pain and pressure, she from her worry and anguish because of what he was going through.

Very soon Naomi mentioned that the deep relaxation, and the new sense of peace and tranquility they were getting through E.F., had added an uplifting fresh dimension and depth. This greatly improved their relationship which had naturally been strained and under siege due to the constant harassment of Douglas's illness. I learned that their sexual activities, "wonderful" before the illness, had ceased because of his constant distress. (Of course this is not true with all forms of cancer.)

Without fully realizing it, until the frank and open discussion with me, they had both missed terribly the comforting feeling of intimacy which sex had provided previously. I suggested that this could be recaptured through fantasizing during the E.F. float. I instructed them in trying this procedure.

In the alleviating state of Erotic Focus, they were to lie closely together comfortably, preferably nude. They would gently stroke each other (he only if he possessed enough strength at the time), recalling in their minds and in spoken words good, enduring memories of sexual and other pleasures. They found that they derived enormous enjoyment from the vivid recollections. "I saw my beloved Doug smile for the first time in months," Naomi told me.

They said they had come to look forward to repeating

the soothing and enlivening experience several times daily and before sleep, and sometimes if they awakened during the night. "We always recall additional 'memories,' some real, some imagined, I suppose," Naomi said. "In any case, this fantasizing, if you will, has brought us a glorious sense of intimate togetherness and sexuality once more. Also, in caressing him softly all over, I was able to lift Doug's spirits marvelously, and my own. You see, we were sharing, instead of my being a helpless bystander . . ."

I was kept informed that this exaltation and enrichment of their lives continued for many months until Douglas died. Naomi advised me that, after he was gone, similar recollection fantasizing during E.F. helped her to handle her grief and sense of loss.

We can all draw lessons from these two people, to help us make the most of our daily activities, sexual and otherwise, no matter how limited. There is no need to await tragedy before we derive the benefits of fantasy-world reinforcement. We can draw on them to improve our real world here and now.

The Many Functions of Sexual Fantasies

Your use of fantasies—intensified with the aid of Erotic Focus clarification and concentration—can function in a number of different ways for your greater sexual enjoyment. The following listing provides a quick review for your handy reference:

1. Adding Pleasure Repeatedly. You can use fantasizing for extra sexual comfort and gratification in two ways: either for imaginative explorations alone and/or with a partner.

However, as mentioned earlier, you should think carefully before exchanging fantasies with a partner. While a shared fantasy can increase ecstasy while making love, if you think it over and realize that your partner may not understand fully and accept your fantasy happily, you might both be better off if you keep your imagining to yourself.

2. Partial Substitute for Actions. You can use fantasizing for temporary relief and satisfaction, if desired, when sexual intercourse with a partner must be postponed—that is, while waiting for the real event. Fantasy can add to your anticipation, and also to partial gratification, if your partner is absent for a while, perhaps on a business trip. Or you might be looking forward to a honeymoon, weekend, vacation, or a forthcoming date. You can obtain sexual release, physically or just mentally, through imagining.

Fantasizing may also provide some compensation for not achieving difficult or unattainable goals. It can allow for partial expression and relief from sexual frustration, enabling you to shift and bear the burdensome pressure with greater ease and a more positive attitude.

However, keep in mind that you cannot expect fantasizing to provide *full* gratification of sexual desires. Fantasies are not a totally fulfilling substitute for active living and wholehearted participation.

3. Creative Enrichment. As we saw in the case of Diana, earlier in this chapter, our minds and our thinking can become hidebound by self-imposed limitations.

We can become ridden with imagined guilt, constricted by boundaries that we set unnecessarily—and often erroneously—for ourselves. And that can be frustrating.

Creative fantasizing, in the liberating state of Erotic Focus, can free our imaginations. You can draw on the inventiveness which each of us possesses, as Diana did. The result can be "creative enrichment," which you can utilize for comparable sexual and other benefits. It's all yours for the using.

4. Overcoming Sexual Monotony. It is not uncommon in a marriage, or in any longlasting partnership, for some sexual monotony and boredom to develop. *But if the individuals involved are conscious of this possibility, they can act to prevent routine and tedium from evolving and intensifying.* Sharing fantasies, playing imaginative and arousing games (see the next chapter), can keep a partnership fresh and increasingly enjoyable. Casual encounters, affairs, and relationships are rarely adequate substitutes; they provide only temporary relief and pleasure at best while fantasy can help keep a marriage or other partnership thriving sexually. Such repeated cooperative enjoyment enhances all the other fulfilling blessings in a mutually loving, caring, enduring relationship between two sharing people. I urge you not to pass up the possibilities for yourself.

5. Preparatory Planning. When in your Erotic Focus float, with your thinking free of daily tensions, when you are able to focus well and unhampered, fantasizing revolving around future events and possibilities can be very productive. You'll find that you're better able to plan and rehearse, and to consider alternate modes of approach and action for maximum sexual gains.

In addition, surveying the possibilities in your imaginative and creative state is an aid to reducing and removing anxiety. Previewing through fantasy can help you to cope with and accumulate utmost rewards from new and developing situations.

6. Reviving Pleasant Past Experiences. "Walking down memory lane," is a form of fantasy which recalls happy past occurrences to refresh and enhance the present. Such fond and joyous recollections do not mean "living in the past." Rather they can help you to utilize and repeat former enriching experiences, to improve your outlook and activities right now. This is demonstrated clearly in the case of Naomi and Douglas. It's worth reviewing and then thinking about applying the possibilities in some form for yourself.

Don't Overemphasize Fantasizing

Even though fantasies can be a productive part of "normal" mental and sexual life, as covered here, they can become unhealthy and unsuitable if overemphasized or used in inappropriate circumstances. These are generally referred to professionally as "pathological fantasies," that is, fantasies that are out of the ordinary, or beyond the average norm.

"The Rock Star Fantasy," described earlier, is a very clear example of pathological fantasizing. The woman who spent all her time and most of her money in pursuing a celebrity she'd never met, but had convinced herself without foundation that he loved her, certainly acted far beyond the bounds of normal behavior.

Such excessive fantasizing can be readily recognized—in yourself and in others—as a self-deluding and harmful escape from coping with serious problems that may arise. Some fantasizing can help one temporarily in handling fears, anxieties, shyness, loneliness. But it is not a substitute for solving the unwanted conditions—nor is it ever recommended as a cure, only as an aid.

It frequently happens, with adolescents particularly, that excessive sexual fantasizing can interfere with school work and other activities. With adults it can obstruct and even prevent efficient performance at work and elsewhere—you've probably heard the expression, for instance, "his mind is in his crotch." Living totally or even mostly in a fantasy world must be avoided lest it hinder an individual's social adjustment to real life and effective dealings with real people.

Experimenting with socially unacceptable sexual behavior in fantasy should also be avoided when it veers way out. For instance, a high school girl's imagining her male teacher standing nude with an erection, even though seemingly silly, may be potentially harmful if it interferes repeatedly with the student's ability to concentrate on the academic material covered. Other fantasies which may be undesirable include using force in sexual encounters, violence in homosexual or heterosexual experiences, sadism, and incestuous involvements. Occasional pathological fantasies, like those just touched upon, may serve to release repressed emotions through acting out the situation in the imagination rather than in actuality. But repeated violent or destructive fantasizing can be increasingly disturbing and guilt-provoking to the individual.

Note this well: If you think that your fantasy may be beyond accepted limits, or presently or eventually damaging to yourself or others—STOP. Remember that practically any excess breeds trouble and possible tragic consequences.

In utilizing fantasies correctly and beneficially, as recommended (as well as with other subjects covered here), it is taken for granted that you know, respect, and stay within the boundaries of responsible and acceptable human behavior, or else this book is not for you. Sexual fantasies are meant to give pleasure, and to add an extra, pleasurable dimension to your relationship . . . but should never become destructive to you or anyone else.

8

"SEXPERIMENTATION" FOR EXTRA THRILLS: SEX GAMES . . . KINKY SEX . . . SADOMASOCHISM

If you don't agree that sex should be *fun* as well as loving and fulfilling and ecstatic then this chapter may not be for you. I believe emphatically that each person is entitled to get the most satisfaction and all-around happiness out of life—*and out of sex*—without hurting anybody.

Sex games and fantasies, which have much in common, can add to life's pleasures, as you'll learn further here. All work and no play makes Jack a dull lover; that goes for Jill too. You can be creative and inventive in having sex. If you're in a playful mood, you can get an extra measure of pleasure from the "sport" approach. Improvisation adds spice—as long as you don't do anything dangerous, such as having sex while entangled in frenzied acrobatics on a trapeze, or any activities involving violence, torture, pain.

A delighted patient, Jane, told me after she had been freed from ingrained sexual inhibitions, "Gary and I now love playing sex games. One of our favorites is to make love in a Jacuzzi tub, with the water swirling madly about us. First we both take a minute or so to go into the E.F. float for relaxation and added perceptiveness. Then we play Tarzan—'Me Jane, you Tarzan'—we howl and clinch and grapple and sputter hilariously until we reach monumental orgasms . . . Wow!''

Psychologically Desirable

From the psychological viewpoint alone, playing games has an important function for everyone, starting in childhood and continuing through the adult years, regardless of age. Playing roles, such as the common acting-out by youngsters, helps them ''rehearse'' behavior with which they're not fully knowledgeable or comfortable as yet. It also aids them in experimenting with new demands in living. We all benefit from employing some playfulness, including sex play, throughout life.

As grownups, playing games reflects more than just the ability to have a good time with each other. Many important thoughts are more easily expressed as a joke, and more readily accepted when conveyed with a sense of humor. You'll find that it makes sense and adds to overall enjoyment when you incorporate ''playing games'' at times in relating with another sexually.

From my professional experience I can assure you that those couples, in marriage or otherwise, who have a sense of humor with each other enjoy the closest and most rewarding relationships. I've seen in a great number of cases in my practice that intimate game-playing helps stabilize the partnership, and often provides the opportunity to ventilate sometimes angry or hurt feelings.

It also helps a person to overcome reticence in expressing love, wishes, fantasies that might otherwise be rejected as too intimate or "heavy," or even threatening. Games help us to probe one another's feelings lightly and then deeply, to diffuse conflicts which might otherwise explode damagingly, to bring two people more closely together.

Games help you to "let yourself go." They supply a pleasurable way to ease tension, relieve anxiety, alleviate fears. In these and other ways, playing games can enhance the entire sexual experience, avoiding the possible boredom that may set in due to routine, sameness, excessive regularity.

Having sex should include having *fun,* not every time necessarily, but enough to spice up your sexual life. A male patient, Jonathan, complained to me, "My wife is so damned serious about having sex. When I was away at a business meeting in a distant city recently, I found myself in bed with a lovely woman who cried out as we experimented, 'This is such fun!' " He added plaintively, "How can I convey that attitude to my wife?"

I told him, as I say to you now, "Why wait for her [or him] to take the lead in playing games and getting extra zest from sex? Why don't *you* try being creative and inventive? You don't have to wait for experimental games, as with the woman in that distant city. You can improvise new ways right here at home with your wife.''

He returned with his wife, Kate, and I taught them the Erotic Focus method to help their relaxation and reawakening. I suggested that they consider being more playful and spirited in their sexual approach. Jonathan phoned me a week later and exulted, "It worked—Kate and I are having fun like when we met, and riproaring sex!"

Not only can playing sex games be stimulating and creative, multiplying your sexual pleasures, but this acting out is also closely related to bringing inner wishes alive—by making the fantasies come true happily, at least partly, if not fully.

I suggest that you make up games that fit and will delight you and your partner the most. You'll find that visualizing possibilities on your mind's TV screen while in your E.F. float will generate many bright ideas. You certainly can improvise—for we all usually have more creative ability than we realize or are putting to use—not only in sex but also in other phases of living. You need not have sex in a jacuzzi or hot tub, nor in a bath or shower or swimming pool; apply your own ingenuity and playfulness—enjoy! Here are just a few brief case history suggestions which have sparked more enjoyment for others—and can for you.

Name Games

What's in a name? More gaiety—when it comes to sex. Referring to sexual organs by pet names (as with nicknames for your loved ones) can break down reserve and boost the sense of elation for more joyous intercourse. A giggling patient, whose primary difficulty was not with sex, told me laughingly that she called her husband's penis "Dopey," and he referred to her vagina as "Soapy." Typically, at a late party in a roomful of people, he'd nudge her and murmur, "How about Dopey visiting Soapy tonight?"

This seemingly silly type of byplay can often relieve and transform a tense situation into a happy result, as in this instance: She said that the first time they went "all the way," she had hastily washed her pubic area thoroughly for extra cleanliness. When they made love, he'd been so excited that he had thrust into her quickly—"Actually I pulled him in, I was so aroused." After a few jerky strokes, he had climaxed before she'd had a chance to "get there myself," as she put it. The embarrassing situation could have brought tears, shame, anger in one or both, especially in him as a man who had failed to satisfy. Seeing his stricken face, she pointed to his shriveled penis and giggled, "Dopey!" Then she noticed her own crotch seething with bubbles foamed up due to her excessive cleansing earlier. She gestured, "Soapy!"

Instead of letting recriminations build, they had both roared with laughter, quivering and hugging hysterically. Humor had saved what might have built into a crisis of failure. The nicknames stuck and amused them repeatedly.

Another couple revealed that they had dubbed their organs "Romeo" and "Juliet" during sex play after an evening at the theater. Thereafter, she might say something like, "Juliet is lonely. . . . Where art thou, Romeo?'' Silly? Perhaps. But such fun and games can enhance and strengthen the joining of two people.

Using ingenious names jokingly can diffuse sexual tensions and irritation which might otherwise lead to angry confrontations. Repeated sexual conflicts can break up a good marriage or other relationship. A former patient applied the name game to her sex life with her husband this way:

"Often at the start of intercourse," Rose explained, "Henry would begin rubbing and squeezing my crotch and breasts so roughly that it became painful. I'd yell, 'Henry, not so hard, dammit, that hurts!' He'd get upset and get soft. Then one time I said gently, 'Hens . . . ease up,' and I made a cackling sound. He smiled and caressed me less severely. Now I only have to say, 'Hens'—and he responds agreeably.

"Similarly . . . at times during my out-of-mind frenzy, I'd grab and crush his penis and balls, and dig my nails into the cheeks of his buttocks. He'd roar, 'Christ, Rose, you're killing me!' I'd be offended and turn away. Then he got the idea to call out, 'Whoa, Rooster!'—and I'd laugh and ease up."

She giggled, "Now our signals for making love are to cackle like a hen, or crow like a rooster, and our pet names are 'Hens' for his penis, and 'Rooster' for me. It not only makes for more fun, but for more uninhibited and satisfying sex."

What's in a name? Consider the possibilities in enjoying sex play more by inventing and bantering with your own.

Playacting for Diversion

Many people keep their sex lives from getting boring or routine by playing roles and thereby spicing up their sex lives. Consider such adventuring for yourself now and then, especially using the freedom of the E.F. float to help move your imagination into high gear.

An instance: An unmarried couple, Vickie and Dan, had been living together for several years. They were devoted to each other, and consulted me because their relationship was beginning to falter. Both said they wanted very much to stay together, but were admittedly finding their sexual intercourse, and their sense of companionship, diminishing.

As part of their joint therapy, I taught them the Erotic Focus method. I suggested that they might be aided by fantasizing during E.F., then acting out their fantasies. They hadn't thought of adding needed variety and improvisation to their sex lives. They now looked at each other with an air of reawakening. Vickie remarked, "Hey, it's as though we've taken out a 'license to experiment.' "

They reported to me blissfully later that they had created the following system which worked marvelously for them: They arranged to "run into each other" at different places at a specified time a couple of days a week "unexpectedly." The site chosen might be at a post office, a store, restaurant, park, at a particular statue—a different spot each time.

They would pretend that they'd never met before,

and would banter and parry while he tried to pick her up. They would adopt different names, identities, occupations, and personalities. They would have a ball assuming and fleshing out their performances as other individuals, in effect participating in the courting game. By playacting, Dan said, "That made it all seem fresh and new. We were flirting again, getting to know the 'stranger.' "

Finally they would wind up in "his" apartment, or "her" pad—always theirs, of course. Dan would turn on some music, serve a drink, begin making passes. She would parry in turn, all of the playfulness building up to exciting intercourse, each still pretending to be the other personality. They said that they had far more enjoyment and better sex in every way than with their past accustomed routine.

"Furthermore," Vickie said, seeming surprised, "we don't tire of playing the games because it's such fun inventing infinite variations."

This constantly creative improvising and acting out different roles repaired their relationship, which became better than ever. Eventually they decided to have a family and were married. They let me know that they continued their playacting game, even after she was pregnant. Why not try it? You too might like it.

Shifting the Scene

You've heard or read before about having sex in a change of scene, I'm sure. I've suggested this to couples a number of times, and it has helped enliven and refresh sexual partnerships in the majority of instances. Kim and Scott, who had been married for less than ten years but already had three young children came to see me because they were finding their relationship dreary, not an uncommon complaint.

Both felt overworked and overburdened by family responsibilities. When I queried each separately about sex, the respones were similar: Kim complained, "I'm too tired most of the time. Intercourse has lost its lift. Can't forget the kids on the other side of the bedroom wall. The thrill has gone—it's dullsville."

As in so many other cases, when I suggested that perhaps they needed a change from family routine, Scott said, "Great, but I just can't afford to take time off from work for a couple of weeks or even one week."

Kim agreed, "We're tied down to giving constant attention to the kids . . . I just don't see any way to do it."

I asked, "Can't you afford the money for an overnight baby-sitter? Or . . . can't you get a relative or friend to stay over for just one evening?"

Wonderingly, "Yes, of course—that's possible—my cousin Joan has offered, but—" Scott looked interested.

First, I taught them to learn to relax and get some relief from the constant daily and nightly pressure by going into the Erotic Focus float several times a day and night, if only for very brief periods. That, they admitted, might provide some immediate breathing room, along with mental and physical refreshment. "I can take a E.F. break when the kids are napping," Kim noted.

As a further step, I suggested, "You both appear to

need desperately a change of scene and environment, even if only for a short period of time. How about a night on the town, perhaps a dinner and some dancing? Then stay over at a motel or hotel . . . something different, a little 'naughty,' perhaps a motel with X-rated movies on the TV set, vibrating beds, the works. Think you'd enjoy that for a transformation of place and pace?''

They were a bit embarrassed, sneaked quick looks at each other, then Scott grinned, ''Sounds kind of foolish . . . but we could try it . . .'' Kim smiled slightly, nodded tentative agreement, and reached out to hold his hand.

She spoke up uncertainly, ''What bothers me is that our lives and our sex together ought to be so sound and satisfying that we shouldn't need any change or extra stimulation . . . right?''

''Think about this,'' I suggested. ''If you were to sit down to eat the same food at every meal, just meat and potatoes, cooked and served the same way in the same place every time, wouldn't you get sick and tired of the food?''

''Of course . . .''

''Would you blame the food itself—or the sameness, the lack of variety, the monotony? Even if you loved meat and potatoes basically, you'd need and want a change, wouldn't you?''

The night on the town and change of scene and environment every couple of weeks worked wonders for their relationship. Perhaps something along the same lines, and variations you dream up yourself, can work for you. Admit it to yourself—there *can* be too much of a good thing, if it becomes humdrum. You can make it a better thing by working at overcoming the boredom of routine where you can learn to enjoy everything more, including sex.

An older, well-to-do couple, pillars of their community, came to see me because, she said, "Since Hector retired, we're getting on each other's nerves—even though we don't want to be apart . . ."

As part of their treatment, I suggested that they try traveling, along with some sexual innovation. I ran into them at a social event a year later. They looked marvelous, very happy. Hector boasted, "We've had wonderful sex in every state of the Union. Now our goal is to start having terrific sex in just about every country in the world."

"Does that mean you don't enjoy intercourse at home?" I asked, laughing.

"Of course we do," the wife replied. "Having been away makes our loving all the better in our own house. We're in our familiar environment, surrounded by our treasured possessions. So we appreciate our home and family and friends and each other all the more. What we have gained is a refreshment of the spirit, and an invigorating new perspective."

Monotony has no special merit in respect to sex or any other phase of living. Creativity often consists of making a good thing better—whether it is an individual pursuit, or marriage, or any partnership. For better sex continually, consider varying the places where you make love, as well as your sexual approaches and actions. Confucius confirmed the value of variety: "They must often change who would be constant in happiness or wisdom."

Let's-Pretend Games

It's common for an acting star to say in an interview, "I was always very shy, basically. I had difficulty expressing myself. But I found that in acting out a part as someone else, I could let go and speak out freely." Strange but true—sometimes we must liberate ourselves from ourselves.

That applies to many individuals and couples who can have sex more freely and rapturously—enjoying better sex—by pretending to be someone else. Here are some examples from my professional experience which may spur some creative ideas for you . . . if you'd care to try some "let's-pretend" sex games.

Prince and Prostitute. One couple I saw expressed concern because their upbringings were so straitlaced that they weren't getting enough pleasure from sex. They were intrigued by the idea of pretending to be other characters in the bedroom—as a means of breaking their confining puritanical mold. I taught them E.F. as an aid.

When they returned a week later, they appeared much happier, were smiling and at ease as they entered. Gail reported their proceedings when having sex: "First we'd both go into the Erotic Focus float to help free ourselves from our usual inhibiting restrictions. Then we'd have fun making up the 'characters' we'd pretend to be that night."

"A favorite," Philip told me, "is a make-believe that we call 'The Prince and the Prostitute.'" He described the action. "I'd dress up in evening clothes. Gail would put on patent leather high-heeled shoes, red net stockings with long lacy can-can garters. She'd bought them especially as costuming. She'd top that with a slinky low-cut dress and long black gloves."

He grinned in recollection. "Now she'd paint her mouth blood-red and overemphasize her makeup, deep purple eye shadow, long artificial eyelashes—the works. Then she'd do a slow, sensuous striptease for 'the Prince,' and we'd wind up in a sexual frenzy on the floor, our clothes scattered all over the place—we couldn't even make it to the bed!"

As often happens with make-believe to shed inhibitions, after a few sessions of "Prince and Prostitute," they agreed that they'd been freed by the overwhelming enjoyment of their orgasms. Gail said contentedly, "We didn't have to play games anymore, so we gave up the improvisations. We had learned that we could always return to let's-pretend now and then if we felt the need or desire for extra stimulation." You always have that option too, of course.

Master and Maid. An amusing twist was described to me by Gerry, who said that she and her live-in partner, Frank, would dream up games individually, and then invite the other to join in. One of their favorites became "Master and Maid." She devised the basic game plan but felt somewhat timid at first about suggesting the performance, so she used her ingenuity and sent him this note which she placed on the table in the entrance hall of their shared home:

"Dear Frank . . . I'm in the mood for playing different roles tonight. Here is the scene: I'm the maid in the house, and you are the master. Your wife is on vacation with the kids. I'll be wearing a very, very, very short uniform, if any. You'll hardly be able to resist . . . and will try to seduce me while I'm serving dinner to you. Anything can happen, and probably will.

Your humble servant—
[signed] Miss Geraldine

P.S. Please indicate your choices regarding the presentation (check one of the boxes below):

( ) Accept gladly.
( ) Not tonight, Geraldine; I'll take a raincheck.
( ) This doesn't send me . . . let's collaborate on
     another plot.

Like others, Gerry and Frank found that they were more relaxed and creative when they began the proceedings by getting into the E.F. float together. "Helps us move into the most playful mood," Frank explained. Soon they enjoyed very much playing a number of different sex games. Their intimacy deepened . . . "We feel closer than ever," Gerry commented, "and more giving to each other."

Superman and Wonder Woman: Patricia and Howard found that they were getting greater enjoyment from sex when—for variety now and then—they took on the parts of what they referred to as "Superman and Wonder Woman," complete with improvised costumes like those worn by the TV actors. They'd figure out a plot beforehand. "That plotting was a lot of fun in itself," Patricia declared, smiling in recollection.

"The script usually went smoothly like this," she went on. "I'd get into a 'dangerous' situation with 'the villain,' Howard, pursuing me—some Wonder Woman! He'd be about to attack and destroy my virtue. Hearing my calls for help, Superman (Howard changing roles) would 'fly' to the rescue and then battle and chase away the awful menace (himself). Saved, I'd hug my hero, and he'd reciprocate. It always turned into passionate lovemaking.'' She added, ''Sounds pretty ridiculous, but it worked every time.''

Variety the Spice of Sex Play. If you like change and diversions, you might like to try sexual playacting. Your creativity can devise infinite variations—whatever appeals to you. Other improvisations described to me by patients include ''Gigolo and Patroness,'' and ''Samson and the Amazon''—a pseudo professional wrestling match between the male and female pair.

One couple who delighted in fancy dining alone would dress formally on ''party night''—with one sexy variation: He would don black tie and tails, but forget his shorts and trousers. She'd put on a flowing gown, and nothing else. They said that they rarely finished the champagne and food before rushing off to the bedroom.

Pretending and improvising is intriguing, adds much extra sexual pleasure for some. Others don't go for performing imaginary plots and characterizations, prefer to take their sex ''straight.'' *Chacun á son gout:* Each to his own taste.

Do . . . but don't overdo. Keep in mind this caution that sex games should bring fun and pleasure, and therefore they must always be carried out with both parties in full agreement. Neither person must ever be forced or coerced into doing something that is not fully acceptable or pleasurable. Whatever games you decide upon should never involve physical or emotional danger to either party, nor to anyone else. Beyond that, practically anything goes.

To get the most from sexual game-playing here's the simple procedure:

1. Discuss and create the game that you both feel you most enjoy playing (put your imaginations to work either before or during E.F.).

2. Go into the Erotic Focus float, as you have learned to do.

3. While in the E.F. float, project on your inner screens the choreography of what you would like to enact.

4. Go to it—inventively, joyously, ecstatically!

Kinky Sex

Some of the literal synonyms for "kinky" include: "twisted . . . perverse . . . weird . . . quirky." Those terms definitely highlight a difference between kinky sex and sex games. In the "games," the basic accent is on sexual fun and joy, as you've noted in the preceding descriptions. "Kinky sex" goes beyond, into more complex experimentation. How far you venture, if at all, hinges on what appeals to you personally, strictly your own choice.

The lure of kinky sex might be likened to that of speeding dangerously on a well-traveled highway, perhaps at 80 miles or more per hour in your car. Obviously you'd be exceeding the speed limit for a possible extra thrill. That could hardly be categorized as either safe or sensible or healthy. Yet some individuals take the risk.

One must be careful, if attempting far-out twists that could be classified as kinky sex, about the possibility of undesired consequences. To understand the contrast with sex games, reflect on the following "kinky sex" performance described to me in an office visit by Abby and Jim. They called one of their typical kinky sex encounters "Master and Slave"—a "bondage" enactment.

"In one version," Jim began, "Abby would be the slave and I'd play the master. I'd 'force' her to strip, pulling off her clothing piece by piece while she screamed in seeming protest . . ."

"He'd throw me on the bed," Abby interjected, "and take off everything but his shirt—all part of his dominance."

Jim went on, "I'd tie her to the bedposts with make-believe ropes, pulling the invisible knots hard and very tight, grunting with muscular effort. With her immobilized, I'd pretend to grip a long leather snake whip. I'd swing the whip viciously with my right hand, yelling out cruelly with each stroke, slapping the bed alongside her body hard with my left hand every time the lash would have cut into her naked back—" He added quickly, "Of course, the nonexistent whip couldn't really harm her . . ."

I asked Abby, "How does the 'Master and Slave' enactment affect you?"

She spoke frankly, her face fixed in a frown of reminiscence, "It gives me a special sexual kick—it does. The sense of danger and cringing from injury adds a certain sexual spice. I let my imagination go—I start twisting and screaming, feeling it in my gut. That excites me, and affects Jim in turn, adding to his fever.

Soon we're grappling—he's pretending to pound me with his fists, me howling for help—"

"I never hurt her," Jim threw in emphatically.

"No . . ." she was hesitant, "not physically . . ." She paused, thinking about her comment. She continued, "Jim finally overcomes my struggles, grips me hard with his hands until I'm subjugated—then he thrusts into me brutally. Fighting, wrestling, plunging against each other—we both burst into terrific orgasms."

She stopped, breathing raggedly, then she added, "Sometimes we'd turn the plot around, and he'd be the slave and I the master. That was pretty intriguing too, although I couldn't work up as much of a threat as he did—he's stronger, of course."

Her voice quavered, "But—lately I've been really scared. Jim was becoming rougher each time, and then he began to talk about using an actual whip—he even bought one—"

"I wouldn't actually hit her with it," he protested.

She went on, ignoring him, her eyes fixed on me, pleading for understanding, "I've been waking up in the night with screaming nightmares, feeling that my body was bleeding, my bones crushed—"

"That's unreal," Jim interrupted. "You know I'd never actually whip or hurt you. I just thought that using a real, solid prop, slamming the whip into the sheets a couple of inches from you—certainly not on your body—that would, like, add more reality. And we'd both get more of a charge out of the act, even more sensational orgasms, see?"

"I know Jim loves me," Abby mumbled. "The proof is his agreeing to come with me to see you when I said I was fearful about where all this kinky carrying-on might lead. Frankly, I'm scared—terrified! What do you think?''

I pointed out to Abby and Jim that her nightmares were urgently signaling, warning that she was in panic about exceeding the boundaries where pleasure turns into terror. The participation and pleasure in kinky sex then becomes one-sided—*a sure stop signal*.

Recognizing Abby's feeling of uneasiness or a vague sense of physical threat, I explained to them, as to you now, that sexual activity cannot be labeled specifically ''moral'' or ''immoral.'' Much depends on what each participating individual wants, how they feel about it mutually. In some cases, relating sexually with activities that are a little kinky can be acceptable and even helpful. It may aid the person in relieving pressures due to rigidity and tightness within oneself—about letting go some in any area of living.

In Abby's case, for example, as she narrated, the kinky sex she practiced (there are any number of forms, as your imagination can conceive) provided special release for Jim, and ''terrific orgasms'' for her. But the balance, whatever he was gaining from the aberrant experimentation, tipped over threateningly toward the negative when fear and terror began to terrorize her dreams, inflicting mental anguish—and possibly worse if she hadn't called a halt.

Infinite Variations

The term kinky sex can cover any number of forms of experimentation and activity. These include unusual and distorted positions during intercourse, quirky oral and anal sex explorations, dangerous bonding practices, urinating or defecating on the partner, inappropriate use of vibrators (not especially "kinky," unless used in extraordinary ways) and other devices. Further variations involve group sex, swinging sex, exchanging partners and other diversifications.

The same fundamental forms of erotic playacting are usually involved in both "kinky" and "games"—that is, taking on such roles as student-and-teacher, prostitute-and-customer, actor-and-ingenue. Again, it's a way of letting oneself go by becoming someone else in active performance, as if disguising yourself by wearing mask and costume (or nothing at all).

But only you can decide what the boundaries are in "games" and "kinky" sex for your own participation. What would be acceptable to someone else may be detestable to you. That applies to most human conduct. One danger when venturing further sexually lies in guarding against ever allowing yourself to be pressured into trying or doing something that you strongly *don't want to do*. I urge you to respect your own intuition and to act or stop accordingly. The summary of guidance tips later in this chapter can be helpful in making your individual decision.

In any kind of sexperimentation, *self-respect* should be

a key issue of which you always should be aware. If your conduct brings on an overpowering sense of shame, if within you cringe in self-loathing at your present or projected actions, I urge you strongly to stop. You owe it to your mental and emotional health to pause and give the matter a great deal of thought before proceeding any further. Whatever course you take then should be your carefully considered decision, not the result of prodding pressure by anyone else.

One test of whether you are abusing or debasing your valued and supportive sense of self-respect is to ask yourself: "Does this particular activity have a depersonalizing effect on me? Does it give me the feeling of being used?" If the answer is *yes* to either question or both, that's a warning of possible or probable damage, temporary or even enduring. Such debasement can be highly injurious to your psyche, to your essential inner being.

Please recognize a vital difference that I call *softcore* versus *hardcore* kinkiness. I define the aim of softcore kinkiness as adding pleasure to sexual activity, as a mutually gainful experience between two people who respect each other. In contrast, hardcore kinkiness generally incorporates hard-driving procedures lacking a light, spontaneous, playful approach. Furthermore, hardcore kinkiness often embodies the risk of physical harm and pain, spilling over into sadomasochism.

As a special warning—it's particularly dangerous to engage in kinky sex with strangers or even with casual acquaintances. This should be obvious, but apparently many take the risk, as attested by repeated reported tragedies. In kinky, as well as any sexual intercourse with someone unknown, there is greater danger of acquiring venereal or other disease, of course—something you might forget in the heat of the stimulating encounter.

There is also extreme peril in engaging in any strangulation or choking routines which, unfortunately, are not uncommon. Even someone you believe you can trust can lose self-control at the peak of excitation, particularly during orgasm—with tragic consequences, choking a partner to death involuntarily.

Another important caution—beware of letting yourself become *addicted* to extreme, hardcore forms of sex. Your attitudes can become twisted through habitual way-out erotic behavior, just as a junkie becomes dominated by the need for hard drugs. You might then find yourself bypassing affectionate, caring lovemaking as being "too tame."

You *can* change if you keep checking yourself about not seeking extra and accelerating thrills constantly, and thus turning into a slave of habit. You must constantly guard against going overboard with extremes of experimenting. And you must never lose a lighthearted, playful attitude about sexual adventuring.

Kinky sex frequently utilizes weird props and costuming which become *fetishes*—items bringing on habitual erotic responses. Typical examples are a blazing orange wig, or spangled G-string (yes, by a man as well as by a woman), or patent leather, spike-heeled boots worn during intercourse every time. Here, again, there is little potential harm if the objects are worn playfully. But when an individual, yourself or the other party, can become aroused *only* through use of the fetish, that's another warning signal: *beware*.

Sadomasochism

Sadomasochism, an apparently increasing phenomenon, is commonly referred to by some as "S-M." It's revealing to break down the derivations of the term:

Sadism—"The association of sexual satisfaction with the infliction of pain on others."

Masochism—"An abnormal condition in which sexual excitement and satisfaction depend largely on being subjected to abuse or physical pain, whether by oneself or by another."

Sadomasochism combines the two, both based on the inflicting of *pain*—physical, mental, emotional, or all three (closely related to each other)—either pain administered by someone else upon you or you against yourself, or pain imposed by yourself on somebody else. Torture is frequently involved. All forms are based on one primary effect: *pain*.

There are a number of S-M "sex shops" which sell a wide variety of items, simple or complicated, for use in sadomasochistic practices. There will always be a small percentage of people attracted by sadomasochism as they search for ever-increasing thrills in sex and other areas. The fact that others take the risk does not justify use or experimentation by you if you don't want it.

My straight-out advice is that you shun most sadomasochistic experimentation and practices. If you "take a chance," the results can be severely damaging, destructive physically and psychologically.

Tips for Maintaining Balance in Sexperimentation

No matter how much self-restraint you have usually, realize that you may not be able to hear that warning inner voice or heed its admonitions when passion is roaring through your body and brain.

The following checklist can help you avoid trouble and even tragedy before they may occur:

- If sexperimentation involves pain, torture, potential physical or psychological damage to yourself, or to your partner, *avoid it*.
- Mutual agreement by both parties is essential, with neither exhorting and compelling the other to do anything unwanted. The result of such pressure is often resentment and blame *after the act*.
- A clear stop signal should be agreed upon ahead of time, so that either one will know exactly how to call a halt to the proceedings . . . and the other will understand and *stop*.
- Don't give in to peer pressure or any other kind of coercion pushing you to engage in any sexual activity against your will. Don't yield to assertions that "Everybody does it" or that "Today's society demands it." You are not "everybody." You are not a "carbon copy." You are not "society." You're an independent, thinking *individual*, with the right and volition to make your own decisions about your personal conduct.

- Respect and self-respect are keystones of sexual conduct. If a specific, questionable sexual activity will diminish your respect for yourself, you'd better bypass it, to guard against psychological damage to yourself. If you think you might feel guilty or depressed afterward, that's a *"no" warning*.

- Sexperimentation with strangers or even with casual acquaintances can be dangerous, carrying an added threat of violence and increased disease hazards—definitely *should be avoided*.

- The natural state of man is joy—that's the statement on a decorative plaque in Samm Baker's office—and a reminder to you too that your approach to sexperimentation should be naturally relaxed, playful, joyous, caring, loving—*for greatest pleasure and deepest gratification*.

- Beware of pushing your body beyond its physical limits in strenuous sexual contortions . . . *if it hurts, STOP!*

- If weird sexual activity is the only type that a partner wants with you, consider ending the relationship . . . or encourage the partner to go for professional help. One-dimensional kinky or sadomasochistic practices can become *obsessive, erotically confining, and inherently dangerous*.

- Be candid and open with your partner about sexperimenting, sharing mutual creativity and elation in adventuring. If you can't be frank with a partner, then there's probably a flaw in the relationship worth investigating and correcting to get the *utmost from sex for you both*.

- Thoughtfulness, good sense, clear communication

are valuable guidewords in aiding you to benefit the most from your sexuality.

Taking exceptional risks in sexperimentation can hurt you and others.

9

SIMPLE SEXUAL EXERCISES FOR MORE SEXUAL PLEASURE . . . FOR WOMEN . . . FOR MEN . . .

"Special exercises for sex?" A couple consulting me repeated that skeptically when I made the suggestion to them. The man, Russ, looked doubtful. "Sounds like a gimmick. How can special exercises possibly increase our enjoyment of intercourse?"

"By strengthening a specific muscle area," I explained. "As everyone knows, certain repeated actions can build up particular muscle masses—in the arms, thighs, and so on."

They nodded agreement.

"It's accepted today," I emphasized, "that *proper* exercising and activity help condition the body and upgrade a person's health in general. All-over functioning usually improves. When it comes to the sexual organs, it can be desirable for many who care, even essential for a good many women and men, to strengthen the PC *[pubococcygeal]* muscle.''

I pointed to the PC muscle, the shaded area in the much simplified chart of the female pelvic area, as reproduced here:

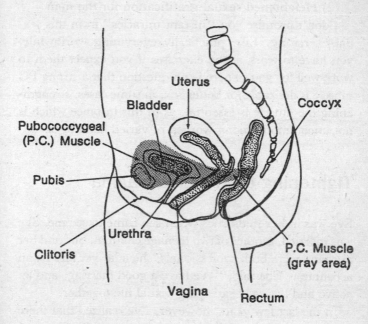

Note that the PC muscle, in relation to the uterus and vagina, is in a position to support the penis and *enhance sensation for the man* during insertion of the penis through the vagina. In addition, and very important, a strong PC muscle brings female nerve endings, and cells sensitive to pressure, close to the penis during penetration. *That intensifies the pleasure of the woman.*

The exercises which you'll be able to learn here and perform readily, if you wish, are designed to strengthen the PC muscle. The double benefit of a strong muscle for the person in normal health, desiring better sex, makes these benefits possible:

(1) Greater sexual arousal for the woman.

(2) Heightened sexual gratification for the man.

I don't promise you "instant miracles" from this sexual exercising. Like practically everything worthwhile, you have to work at the exercises if you expect them to work well for you. There is no question that a strong PC muscle is desirable for better sex; in some cases, strengthening the muscle is essential, as in this instance which is not uncommon among women of varied adult ages:

Tightening the Flaccid Vagina

Eve was in her midforties when she came to see me. She was married, mother of two teenage children. She and her husband were both professionals, she a lawyer and he an accountant. She said, "We have a good marriage and an active and basically satisfying sexual life together."

In the last few years, however, Eve realized that there was a physical change in her sexual organs. She felt sure that her vagina had become much looser and less sensitive, and had lost its "grip" on her husband's penis.

Disturbed, she visited a plastic surgeon who affirmed that her vagina had become flabby, and required tightening. She'd had similar surgery five years before, and results were satisfying, but the tightness had dissipated after a year. She had some recent bladder incontinence (lacking full control). Her surgeon attributed it not only to the physical problem of having weak muscles but also to emotional pressure and overload at work.

Rather than proceed with surgical repair again now, the surgeon referred Eve to me for counseling. In our discussion about the case, he confirmed the findings of his examination: "The patient's vagina has very weak muscle tone; she could not squeeze around the inserted finger during the examination."

Eve had a total of three sessions with me, one with her husband present. It became clear that she was a prime candidate to learn the sexual exercises that will be taught here. I explained to her the anatomy and physiological functioning in respect to her vaginal problem, and how regular sexual exercising could restore the tightness of her vagina.

The ultimate muscular strengthening in the area, I emphasized, would probably improve the sexual enjoyment of her husband and herself. In addition, the urinary incontinence would very likely be cured. I taught her the exercises, along with the Erotic Focus method, and how to combine the two for best results (as instructed in this chapter).

Intelligent and eager, Eve adopted the program energetically. She practiced all the exercises faithfully. Intent on gaining the quickest possible improvement, she repeated the exercise routine up to twenty times a day initially. Then she continued the methodology three times daily, right up to now, as part of the everyday activities. *She and her husband are delighted by the results.*

While you may consider Eve's condition somewhat extreme, realize that—even from the teens in many cases—the PC muscle may not be as strong as it should be for most effective functioning. I assure you that the sexual exercises can be helpful for general top conditioning too, as with general exercising for all-around top body fitness and performance.

Exercises Developed for Repair, Strength, Pleasure

Genital exercises were first described by Dr. Theodore Van de Velde in the 1920s, and later from 1948 on by Dr. Arnold Kegel, a noted urologist. Such exercises were developed initially by Dr. Kegel for patients who suffered from urinary incontinence due to genital problems *(trauma)* secondary to childbirth.

The routines were applied also for the treatment of *stress* incontinence, a weakening of the urethral sphincter and resulting escape of urine when bearing down, sneezing, coughing, or while having orgasms. But it has long been known that strengthening the PC and other muscles around the vaginal, pelvic, and anal area *(perineal muscles)* could improve a woman's sexual sensitivity. Also it could even promote orgasm in some women who had been unorgasmic previously.

In respect to sexual intercourse, many women who had good control over their orgasms learned how to tense the vagina and the perineal muscles voluntarily for this specific purpose: The woman can achieve muscle mastery, as desired. She can gain the ability to help initiate and/or intensify the orgasmic experience for *herself*, and for her *partner* as well. *The exercises can help you do the same,* a definite asset for better sex.

Who Should Do Sexual Exercises?

If you fit one or more of the following categories, you are a candidate to benefit from the PC sexual exercises:

1. *Any woman who is not now aware* of the importance of the perineal muscles and who wants to learn how to strengthen them so that she can improve her (and her partner's) sexual enjoyment (as exemplified in the case history cited).

2. *Women with genital slackening* due to childbirth and/or faulty postpartum (after childbirth) or other gynecological procedures (see ''Tightening the Flaccid Vagina'').

3. *Women with injury* to the vagina, due to a variety of physical or surgical trauma.

4. *Women with thinning of the vagina* due to certain changes during menopause . . . and/or other causes which alter the hormonal balance, such as may happen after hysterectomy (but not necessarily).

5. *Women with urinary stress incontinence* (some loss of urine when bearing down, coughing or sneezing, or during orgasm). Incontinence, when it occurs, is usually secondary to genital weakening after childbirth, or vaginal atrophy (wasting or thinning of the vaginal walls). This may lead to resulting atrophy of the sphincter muscle of the urethra opening (see urethra canal position in earlier pelvic area diagram).

6. *Women who have sexual problems* ranging from vaginismus (spasm of the muscles surrounding the entrance of the vagina), anorgasmia (difficulty or inability to experience orgasms), to diminution or lack of vaginal sensitivity.

Sexual exercises can generally be helpful in overcoming and correcting such difficulties, by strengthening the PC muscle.

Locating Your PC Muscle

Here are three accepted ways for you to try (your choice, or proceed with all three) in order to locate your PC muscle, and to test it for strength and efficiency. The first way is most acceptable for many women, but testing with all three ways provides the best check. Although No. 1 can suffice if you don't like the other two ways, you can have your partner cooperate and help in methods No. 2 and No. 3—it's up to you.

No. 1. While urinating normally, try to stop the flow of the urine midstream by squeezing internally to tighten the urinary tract (you're actually squeezing your PC muscle). If your muscle is in relatively good condition, *you will be able to stop the flow instantly and completely.* If your PC muscle is weak, the flow will continue until the bladder is empty. In the latter instance, that's a clear signal that your PC muscle definitely needs strengthening—for better sex as well as for other desirable functioning.

No. 2. Lie down on your bed (by yourself or with your partner to assist). Insert your finger into your vagina (or have your partner do so with his finger). Touch with a little pressure *(palpate)* the middle of your vagina (that is, about halfway in). You may feel a slightly uncomfortable sensation from the pressure (don't press hard, just gently) . . .

Now, tighten your vagina around the inserted finger and you'll find that the slightly uncomfortable sensation disappears. Instead you'll feel a rather pleasant effect in that area. (It is one of the outmoded anatomy myths, now known to be untrue, that the vagina is completely insensitive except around the entrance [introitus], so don't be misled.)

At this moment, with your finger in place, and you tightening your vagina, *you'll be able to feel the contraction of the PC muscle there.* This is significant: The better the condition of your PC muscle, the tighter the finger will be squeezed, mainly around the second joint of the finger. If the "squeezed" sensation is very light, your PC muscle is flaccid and you could benefit considerably from strengthening it, getting it in shape for better sex, as well as for other desirable normal functioning.

No. 3. When you are having an orgasm, insert your finger into your vagina and/or anus as you are coming (or have your partner insert his finger). Again, if your PC muscle is in good condition, the inserted finger will feel the contraction of the muscle. If no contraction is felt, or only a very weak one, it means that your PC muscle is lacking in *muscle tone* (vigor, resilience, tension)—which, as noted, can be due to effects of childbirth, hormonal changes, or inadequate use and exercise.

Keep in mind that your PC muscle, as with any muscle, benefits from repeated, routine, proper exercising.

How to Use the E.F. Technique with PC Muscle Exercises

Combining the Erotic Focus method with the PC exercises produces more effective exercising and results in these two primary ways:

1. You are relaxed all over, without tension, an essential for most productive exercising.

2. You benefit from *E.F. focused concentration* for performing the exercises correctly . . . and on getting the most from the exercising.

Here's how to use the E.F. method along with PC muscle exercises, most successfully;

A. *Check over the E.F. procedure thoroughly again* (reread Chapter 3) to make sure you know every detail correctly. After a little more practice, make sure you have it all down pat and are enjoying the quick benefits of E.F. Apply the technique to the PC muscle exercises every time you do them.

B. *Read the instructions carefully* for the four PC exercises that follow; go through the motions of each one slowly in order to learn the actions well.

C. *Go into the E.F. float.* In the float, do the exercises, one through four as a routine set. When you finish the set, remain in E.F., take a couple of deep breaths in and out between each set . . . then rerun the exercise sets at least three times altogether. Come out of E.F. at the end of the three or more sets.

NOTE: *If you are doing the PC exercises in public—perhaps in a large, open office, or on a bus—you can use the "Quickie E.F. Relaxation Break" technique, as instructed in Chapter 3.*

There may be a question in your mind now, as I've been asked now and then by a patient, so I'll answer in advance: Yes, you *can* perform the PC exercises without going into the E.F. float. However, being in E.F., as stated at the start of these instructions, gives you the valuable additional advantages of being not only relaxed but also *fully alert and focused* on each step of the actions. Being in the state of E.F., you'll be much more aware of the exercise motions and the pleasant and productive sensations you're enjoying in the process, deep down within you. Furthermore, exercising in the E.F. float (as with all types of exercising) improves your efficiency and brings you the full benefits more rapidly. *As a bonus* you'll find that you are exercising and strengthening all the muscles in the area, not just the PC muscle.

The Four PC Muscle Exercises For Women

POSITIONING YOUR BODY

Use either of these two positions: sitting or lying on your back, as you please—clothed or not. Both positions support your body well, also aid in promoting most attractive, healthful posture all over, an extra benefit of the PC exercises.

Sitting: Sit in a firm (not soft) chair, head and upper body comfortably erect, *never slumped*. With knees and feet a few inches apart, rest your hands on your thighs, palms down.

Lying on Back: Lie on your back on the floor (preferably carpeted, for comfort), or on a firm bed, with your head at ease, and your shoulders flat against the floor, arms resting comfortably near your sides, palms up. Bend your knees up, spaced about four to six inches apart, with feet resting a few inches apart, flat on the floor.

PC Exercise #1: Squeeze-Relax

Pull in the cheeks of your buttocks vigorously, squeezing your PC muscle (which you located previously) for three seconds . . . then relax the muscle for three seconds. Repeat the squeeze-relax actions ten times.

If you find it difficult to squeeze your PC muscle three times at first, do one or two squeezes—and not the full ten repeats if that tires you. Proceed day by day to build up to three squeezes and ten repeats each set. You'll find that the entire routine becomes very easy, and energizing rather than tiring.

PC Exercise #2: Squeeze-Release-Repeat

This is very much like exercise #1, except that you squeeze the PC muscle, release it, squeeze again, then release as quickly as possible. Rerun this action for ten sets—at least three times daily. You'll be able to increase your squeeze-release-repeat speed considerably day after day.

PC Exercise #3: Pull-Hold-Release

Imagine that there is a tampon or penis or finger in your vagina, then *pull it in and hold it in tightly* for three seconds with your PC muscle, then release. Repeat the total actions ten times in each set of the four PC exercises.

PC Exercise #4: Pull-Push-Down-Release

This time *pull inward,* then *push down* as during a bowel movement, but with emphasis on the vagina in pushing down, rather than on the anal area, then release after three seconds. With E.F. focused concentration and practice on the pull-push-down actions, you'll be able to push down on the vagina correctly, thus strengthening your PC muscle as desired. Repeat the actions ten times in each set of the PC exercises.

To keep your PC muscle in top condition for better sex and other functions, repeat each exercise in the set ten times, and rerun the session at least three times daily whenever most convenient for you (upon awakening, midday, and bedtime add up to a good schedule).

After a week or two, as you progress, slowly increase to twenty of each exercise in the set, and you can do each set as often daily as you find time and desire (but consider three times daily a minimum).

You can do the first three exercises practically anywhere without anyone nearby noticing. That is probably true of exercise #4 also, but you be the judge.

If enough time is not always available at every session to go through the entire set of four PC exercises, then do as many as the particular occasion permits. Even a very short period of the strengthening actions is better than none. Of course, doing the full set each time produces the best cumulative result to bring you the very healthful, pleasurable benefits you want and probably need.

I urge you to phone your obstetrician-gynecologist or personal physician beforehand for approval to do the exercises. Please don't fail to do this in any case, but particularly if you've had any medical problems in this area.

If you find this exercising *painful* at any time, Stop— and check with your doctor again.

When beginning the exercises, if you feel any discomfort or tightness in the pelvic area, reduce the number of daily successive actions . . . but don't abandon the exercises (do stop if there is *pain*). Like any muscle that is being exercised at the start, there may be a little stiffness at first, which will disappear very soon.

Just realize very definitely that it is important to keep your PC muscle, like others, in tone. You'll find that the exercises become as much a daily habit as brushing your teeth (but more pleasurable), and should be continued for your lifetime. The rewards, especially for better sex, are multiple and *most enjoyable year after year!*

PC Muscle Exercises for Men

Although the PC muscle exercises here were developed principally for women, there is increasing medical and clinical evidence that men are likely to benefit considerably from a strong PC muscle in these three ways specifically:

1. Enhances the strength and duration of the erection, as much as the perineal muscles (one of which is the P.C. muscle) are involved.

2. Aids more efficient thrusting during intercourse.

3. Offers benefits for men afflicted with some degree of stress incontinence (leakage) . . . prostate problems . . . postsurgical complications (prostatectomies, rectal repairs, etc.).

As recommended earlier for women, I urge men also to do this: Call your physician, describe briefly the PC muscle test and exercises, and get the doctor's approval before proceeding (undoubtedly the okay with be forthcoming).

Locating and Testing the Male PC Muscle

With the male anatomy, do the following (quite similar to test No. 2 for women):

Lie down on your bed (by yourself or with your partner to assist). Insert your finger into your rectum several inches (or have your partner do so with her finger). Touch with a little pressure *(palpate)* with your finger; you may feel a slightly uncomfortable sensation from the pressure (don't press hard, just gently) . . .

Now tighten your rectum around the inserted finger . . . and any uncomfortable feeling will disappear, replaced by a rather pleasant effect in the area.

At this moment, with your finger in place, and you tightening the rectal passage internally, *you'll be able to feel the contraction of the PC muscle there.* Note this carefully: The better the condition of the PC muscle, the tighter the finger will be squeezed. If the "squeezed" sensation is very light, your PC muscle is flaccid, and you could benefit considerably from strengthening it.

Exercises to Strengthen the Male PC Muscle

Read in detail instructions for the four PC muscle exercises given for women to strengthen the PC muscle. *Follow the same directions,* simply substituting "rectum" for "vagina," where noted. Perform the set of exercises as per instructions—a minimum of three times daily.

Soon, by testing further, you should feel a strengthening of your PC muscle in the tightness around your finger in the rectum test. You should gain definite benefits in greater enjoyment of better sex—as your partner should too.

To Exercise or Not to Exercise?

As with all healthful, correct exercising—with the real multiple potential benefits—the *doing* of the simple PC muscle exercises is up to you specifically. Neither I nor anyone else can exercise for you. Whether you're a pauper or a multimillionaire, it's your body—you must do the exercises yourself.

Since you are taking the time to read this book, I believe that you are sufficiently motivated to do the exercises and gain the rewards in better sex and other functions.

10
IMPROVING WOMEN'S ORGASMS; OVERCOMING ORGASMIC DYSFUNCTIONS

This chapter concentrates on helping every woman get the greatest pleasure from orgasms and aiding the woman who has never had an orgasm—or thinks she may never have come to orgasm—to achieve her goal. This chapter will also give assistance to any woman who has experienced orgasms, but with some sort of difficulty. The simple, easy-to-learn procedures you will learn here incorporate the Erotic Focus technique. Please remember that any significant change in your sexual functioning and any sexual dysfunction (such as the primary problems described on the following pages) should always be brought to the attention of your family physician or gynecologist.

Anorgasmia

Anorgasmia is "the inability to come to orgasm." Women who have sexual problems used to be called "frigid." The term is negative and misleading. While *frigidity* literally means "extremely cold," women who suffer from sexual inhibitions are not necessarily cold, hostile or neurotic. They are merely afraid of sex, or not attracted to their partners. They can be warm and loving, sexual and sensuous. Since the term "frigidity" has a very negative and incorrect connotation, I prefer not to use the word "frigidity" when referring to anorgasmia.

The inability by a woman to have an orgasm (defined as "the apex and culmination of sexual excitement") is the most common female *psychosexual*—that is, *not organic*—dysfunction. The treatment here covers psychosexual anorgasmia rather than that due to identifiable diseases and physical disorders. As with all treatment of sexual dysfunctions, *organic causes must be ruled out first by thorough physical examination by a qualified physician.* If the problem is not organic, it has been my experience with my anorgasmic women patients, affirmed by reports of other qualified sex therapists, that anorgasmia is the easiest sexual dysfunction to treat and remedy for gratifying and enduring success.

If you never come to orgasm (*primary* anorgasmia), or do not experience orgasm readily (*secondary* anorgasmia), it helps to realize that you are not alone in your dysfunction—not by a long shot. Figures vary, but here are the generally accepted percentages:

10 percent of all women never reach orgasm

10 percent are not able to climax with a partner, but are able to come to orgasm through masturbation

50 percent of women reach orgasm with intercourse plus *clitoral* stimulation (the clitoris is the small erectile organ at the upper part of the opening of the female genital organs)

30 percent have orgasm during intercourse *without* any clitoral stimulation.

In the past, sexologists differentiated inaccurately between *vaginal* and *clitoral* orgasm. Now it is pretty well understood by students of human sexual behavior that the final physiological response is much the same— regardless of the beginning point, whether through stimulation of the vagina or clitoris, or both.

Women differ considerably in how easily they reach orgasm. If only 30 percent of all women reach orgasm through intercourse *without additional stimulation*, then 70 percent of women have some kind of dysfunction, minor to major. They can improve their orgasmic satisfaction, and generally overcome their problems, through the Erotic Focus technique and the methodology taught here.

Most Common Causes of Anorgasmia

While all causes of common psychosexual anorgasmia are not fully known, the most likely roots involve what are referred to professionally as "intrapsychic, interpersonal, cultural, and learned-behavioral factors." In more common terms, these are the usual roots of anorgasmia:

CAUSES OF PRIMARY ANORGASMIA (WOMEN WHO HAVE NEVER EXPERIENCED ORGASM)

- cultural
- educational
- learned behavior
- moral
- religious
- gender confusion
- homosexual orientation (anorgasmic with person of other sex, but possibly orgasmic with partner of same sex)
- traumatic past events such as incest, rape, homosexual experience, physical trauma due to illness or surgery

CAUSES OF SECONDARY ANORGASMIA (WOMEN WHO DO NOT EXPERIENCE ORGASM READILY)

- check all the "Primary Causes," plus:
- fear of intimacy
- fear of pregnancy
- infidelity involvement
- infertility
- menopause
- physical illness
- medication with loss of sexual desire due to it
- drug use, including alcohol abuse
- venereal disease
- stress
- fatigue
- depression
- obesity or other eating disorders with changes in body image
- low self-esteem
- anxiety states

TRACKING DOWN THE SPECIFIC CAUSE

It's vital for you to note *which* of these causes, one or more, may be possibilities triggering your personal primary or secondary anorgasmia. Those will be related helpfully later in your Erotic Focus exercises. To help you recognize the particular kind of anorgasmia affecting you, here is a quiz. Answer the following questions with checkmarks at "yes" or "no."

1. Have you *always* failed to have orgasms during intercourse?
   Yes____ No____
2. Do you have orgasms *only occasionally* during intercourse?
   Yes____ No____
3. Do you have orgasms only with a *certain partner . . .* and *not with another partner?*
   Yes____ No____
4. Have you had orgasms for a while with intercourse, followed by *periods of not coming to orgasm?*
   Yes____ No____
5. If you experienced orgasms, *then developed anorgasmia* since that time, have there been *changes* such as
   A. Changes in your *relationship* with the partner?
      Yes____ No____
   B. Changes in your *general health,* or onset of any *specific health problems?*
      Yes____ No____
   C. Changes in your *job* or *home situation?*
      Yes____ No__;b m
   D. *Added worries or stress* about any particular identifiable changes or developments in your life?
      Yes____ No____

In checking your answers to these questions, you are likely to learn that you have *secondary* rather than primary anorgasmia. If your answer to the first question in the listing—that you have *never* experienced orgasm—is a positive yes, then your problem is *primary* anorgasmia, which generally takes longer to correct. Nevertheless, it can usually be overcome with treatment.

If, as is generally the case, in answering all the questions you realize that *you have had orgasms* sometimes—however infrequently—then you probably have *secondary* anorgasmia. This less severe condition usually responds quickly and easily to your Erotic Focus exercises and to the detailed step-by-step techniques in which you will be instructed later in this section.

Characteristics of Most Anorgasmic Women

Many women have problems with orgasm and, unsurprisingly, they all have several characteristics in common. My patients are instantly relieved from understanding this clearly, and I trust that these facts provide encouraging insight for you too—even if your characteristics are not exactly the same as in the examples provided later.

The woman who experiences problems with orgasm usually has a normal sexual desire. She enjoys intercourse, lubricates normally when aroused, but has difficulties reaching orgasm. She achieves a certain level of sexual excitement, but when it comes to "letting go," she is blocked by obstacles in climaxing, overwhelmingly psychosexual in origin.

Women vary considerably as to how much stimulation each may need to reach orgasm. Some women can climax only when they are alone masturbating, but the presence of a partner—in effect an "audience"—makes them feel too inhibited or embarrassed or tense to attain orgasm. Often this type of woman feels that she is taking too long or that her partner will reject her if he has to "work" at getting her to climax.

For many women, who come to orgasm quite easily and with confidence while masturbating, it takes a good deal of clitoral stimulation when together with a partner—but eventually they do come to orgasm.

All too often, a woman who takes a long time to reach orgasm, or who is anorgasmic, *pretends* to have an orgasm because she is embarrassed to communicate the fact of her slowness, difficulty or inability to climax to her partner. Most women in this category could actually come to orgasm if they gave themselves and the partner a chance. Unfortunately, they are usually oversensitive to rejection or criticism, or overanxious to please the partner—and fail to climax. Is that true of you?

Faking the Orgasm

It's extremely important to realize that *faking orgasm usually interferes with developing a good sexual relationship*. In fact, faking orgasm usually tends to make the situation worse.

It is a fact, whether desirable or not, that orgasm has become more important to women over the last twenty years or so. There is no question that the pressure for a woman to have an orgasm every time has been increased and vastly overemphasized.

As a result, women have felt undue obligation to "perform." Often they almost feel "dewomanized" if they don't have multiple orgasms or if orgasm isn't always an ecstatic experience. Understand this fully and definitely: The final phase of sexual intercourse, the orgasm, is important, *but it should be placed in proper perspective in the human experience of having sex*.

The orgasm is *not* the be-all and end-all of sexual pleasure and total reward. Experience it—yes—but don't exaggerate its importance. Don't let anyone (including yourself) put you down if you should fail to have an orgasm, or don't "explode" in multiple orgasms. Nor should you believe empty boasts by anyone of "fantastic multiple orgasms" which may well be downright lies.

For most people, true sexual enjoyment has more to do with *quality*, not quantity: The ultimate in sexual gratification is in the *close, loving relationship between the two partners*.

Experiencing and Understanding Orgasms

An attractive woman patient, Nina, had arranged to see me because she was worried that something might be wrong with her sexually. She was well adjusted, well functioning, in her midfifties. She had an enduring marriage, with two grown children. Her husband had been her only sex partner through over thirty years of marriage. They had a very good relationship with each other, enriched with love and mutual respect.

Nina told me, "I've enjoyed satisfactory sexual intercourse through the years. How often? Oh . . . from two to four times a week, more or less regularly. I like sex with my husband, but I'm not sure I've experienced 'orgasms.' Plus," she went on slowly, "I've become more and more concerned about it because I've read so many articles in magazines about 'multiple orgasms,' and 'clitoral versus vaginal orgasms.' I'm confused."

She continued, explaining her self-doubts, "I've heard so much on television and radio, and read repeatedly in all media to 'Be liberated and assert your right and ability to have orgasms!' Honestly," she emphasized, "I've become very concerned about my own sexuality. Now I must find out from you professionally whether something is wrong with me . . ."

After questioning Nina in detail, it began to appear that she may never, or perhaps rarely, have experienced orgasm—even though she felt that she had an enjoyable and fulfilling sexual relationship with her husband. I told her that, from what she said, she might never have fully developed her sexuality to reach orgasm. "But," I emphasized, "it doesn't mean that you're not 'normal' or not 'sexual.' "

I went on to compare having an orgasm with having a meal. "You can fully enjoy an appetizer, the main dish, a salad, and a glass of wine—without having a dessert. *Orgasm*," I stressed, "is like having a dessert at the end of the meal. If you fully enjoyed the other parts of the meal, you really did not miss out much by not having dessert."

She nodded in agreement, her expression already reflecting relief and reduced tension.

I went on to explain to Nina that if she was curious about "the dessert," that is, the orgasm, I could teach her how to get there, or at least get a feeling about what the hullabaloo was all about. She agreed that she would like to investigate further.

I taught her the Erotic Focus technique, as you have learned—to feel very comfortable and relaxed. I then suggested that after she had achieved thorough relaxation through her E.F. exercises, she might proceed to masturbate while in the Erotic Focus float.

She responded with concern, "But I've never masturbated at all!"

I assured her, "You need not if you don't care to, but you should understand the point here . . ."

I explained that the purpose of the masturbation was to see if she could reach a state of sexual arousal where she felt so excited physically that her pelvic muscles wanted to contract almost irresistibly—and she would then let go and let the orgasm come. I noted that *this sensation of overpowering contraction of the pelvic muscles is the orgasm.*

"For most women," I concluded, "this is an extraordinarily pleasurable sensation." She nodded that she understood.

When she returned for the next session, she told me that she had followed through as I had explained. She stated forthrightly that she had learned the E.F. method . . . then had masturbated. She said, "Yes . . . I experienced that orgasm . . ." She stopped, stayed silent, looking at her hands in her lap.

I asked, "Why do you hesitate?"

"The fact is," she continued slowly, "after the orgasm I felt quite let down . . . and disappointed . . ." I waited.

"From what I had read about orgasms," she said, "I thought that I would hear 'a thousand bells ringing' and—as they claim—would 'feel the earth turning'. . ." She smiled wryly, "But I didn't. That's okay . . . and now I believe that I *have* experienced 'orgasms' a number of times with my husband in the past. But," she shrugged, and now smiled fully, "you are right. That highly touted orgasm is fine, but it's just the dessert and . . . I think I like the main dish better, the closeness and sharing with my husband. I'll enjoy my orgasms when they happen . . . and not really mind if they don't.''

Nina concluded, ''This experience has helped me in many important ways.'' She clarified that she no longer felt the self-defeating pressure to have an orgasm every time, but with Erotic Focus ''I'm going to let go more during lovemaking from now on.'' She said she felt relieved of stress, and ''I know that I'll delight in sexual intercourse even more than before.''

The treatment that helped her so much is explained here in the same detail I taught her—in the following:

Stage-by-Stage Treatment to Correct and Overcome Anorgasmia

The clear, effective treatment which has worked so well in helping many of my anorgasmic female patients to overcome their difficulties divides into two phases:

In the first stage, you—as the anorgasmic woman— are to proceed without involving a partner.

In the second stage, the partner will participate along with you, according to the simple instructions.

PHASE I—WITHOUT A PARTNER

First, you are to practice the Erotic Focus technique thoroughly and repeatedly. After you have gone through the pleasant routine sufficiently so that you have complete confidence about it, move forward to put yourself in the state of Erotic Focus. Now, while in

E.F., ask yourself the following questions . . . and check the answers precisely as they apply to you:

---

1. Are you encountering any problems about your *interest* in having sex?
     YES____ NO____
2. Has there been a *change* in your level of interest?
     YES____ NO____
3. Have any *recent or past events* influenced your interest in sex?
     YES____ NO____
4. Do *fantasies* play a part in your sexual enjoyment?
     YES____ NO____
5. Are there any specific situations, feelings, or attitudes which cause you to *enjoy sex less . . . or not at all?*
     SOME (name them)_____ NONE AT ALL ____
6. How *often* do you have sex . . . and has the *frequency* lessened?
     NO. OF TIMES_____ LESS? YES____ NO____
7. What part of sexual play and intercourse do you *enjoy* most . . . and *not enjoy at all?*
     ENJOY MOST_____ NOT ENJOY_____
8. Do you feel *guilty* about participating in and enjoying sex?
     YES____ NO____
9 . Do you naturally *lubricate well* when you get aroused?
     YES____ NO____
10. Do you *communicate* your sexual desires to your partner?
     YES____ NO____
11. Do you feel comfortable about *asking your partner* to stimulate you?
     YES____ NO____
12. Under what circumstances can you *achieve orgasm,* that is (check):
     By intercourse?____ Manual stimulation?____ Oral sex?____ Vibrator?____ Masturbation?____ Anal sex?____ Other?____

13. Is there anything about your orgasmic response, when you have an orgasm, that *troubles* you?
    YES (WHAT?)_____ NO____
14. What, if anything, *interferes particularly* with your ability to reach orgasm?
    ANSWER_____
15. Are you afraid that having an orgasm means *losing control?*
    YES____ NO____

Important: While in the state of Erotic Focus, feeling free of tensions, helped by focused concentration, and with the confidence of having personal mastery, *you are more intimately in touch with your feelings and thinking.* In this state, your uninhibited thoughts can surface and be revealed more clearly to you.

Furthermore, in your liberated E.F. state, if any of these quiz questions, or any other questions arise in your mind, do this: *Repeat the question or questions to yourself as highlights.* By doing this, you will have already narrowed down your personal problem area.

FOCUSING TO FIND YOUR SOLUTION

Your next step is to *find the individual right answer or answers that apply specifically to your own problem.* You can arrive at the correct findings in the following way: Once you have reduced the number of possibilities, and beamed in on one of the questions, as applying most particularly to your own actions and reactions about sex, go on to the next stage.

Still in the relaxed, illuminating state of Erotic Focus, now imagine that you are looking at a TV or movie screen within your mind. On this screen, *focus on projecting your question,* as a participant in a TV quiz show might see it on a card or board . . .

Now, zooming in on the question on your TV screen in your inner vision, let your brain computer do some work on the subconscious level. As you allow and encourage your deep feelings to come to the surface, permit your brain computer, freed of your usual inhibitions, to gradually *project the right answer on the screen—which will happen* (as you will discover for yourself).

For example, let's center on question #13 as a penetrating insight that you chose as hitting home especially for you. Repeat the query in your mind silently: "Is there anything about your orgasmic response, when you have an orgasm, that *troubles* you?"

In your state of E.F. clarity and freedom, think about this point intensely again. As you concentrate on it, visualizing the words, you will see the question written clearly on the screen inside your mind (just as one "sees" pictures, images and words appearing in dreams).

REVIEWING "PROBLEM SITUATIONS" VISUALLY

What happens next shows you *how the subconscious mind operates naturally.* What your brain computer is doing is reviewing situations where, in the past, you had orgasms . . . exactly how you experienced them . . . how you felt personally about them . . . how your partner responded to your orgasms . . . and other details of the sexual experience. *Try to project actual pictures of the situations as a movie on your inner TV screen . . .*

Gradually the answers will be spotlighted into your conscious realization and will come through clearly to help you, such as (picturing again the actual replay): "Yes, in the past [since you started having sexual intercourse], when I would have an orgasm, I felt physically uncomfortable and could not stand any further thrusting of the penis inside my vagina."

Or the vivid realization and replay might be: "I remember now that during my first relationships, I used to climax relatively quickly, and my boyfriend wanted to continue again and again, but by then *it had become painful for me* and I wanted it all to be over with, to *stop.* . ."

Or perhaps, "Yes, I recall now—though I had forgotten—episodes [replay them on your inner screen] when I was pressured by too urgent caressing and even insertion and I became increasingly upset and resistant deep inside myself and I turned off angrily after I had climaxed in spite of not wanting to . . ."

Thoughts and replays of this nature may surface for you on your inner screen, and your personal problem and blockage will become evident. Now that you know and understand what happened in the past, and it has solidified for you, you are ready to go on to the next step . . .

Using Fantasy in Phase I

Still treating your anorgasmia in Phase I without a partner, I'd like you to contemplate using *fantasy* to increase your desire and to explore systematically exactly what can arouse your sexual feelings, desires, and culmination most surely and fully. You learned a great deal about fantasizing in Chapter 7. Now, here's exactly how to take an E.F. effective fantasy trip.

First, go into the state of Erotic Focus.

Now, again, imagine that you are looking inside your mind at a TV screen or movie screen. As you focus on this screen, project your favorite fantasy—or, if you have never thought about the subject, and have no favorite fantasy, experiment with some of the ones described in this book or make up fantasies of your own.

Consider some of the most popular fantasies as possibilities. These involve images within the mind. Understand, please, that this is not a deviant course. Sexual fantasies are used commonly by a great many people, willfully or simply as part of letting one's imagination roam freely and even creatively. Such fantasies can be used while having sex, or at other times when fantasizing is appropriate and not intrusive.

These fantasies are strictly private, just between you and your imagination. For example, you might visualize yourself now being made love to and making love with the person you love . . . being caressed by the person you love . . . just being held closely by the person you love, kissing, fondling . . .

Other women find it more exciting to fantasize about making love with a stranger . . . with someone of the same sex . . . participating in an orgy . . . mutual oral sex with a particular remote partner . . . having anal intercourse . . . being tied up or other fantasies that are strictly of the imagination.

As with all my suggestions for self-treatment, there is no pressure from me that you *must* fantasize—if that is distasteful to you for one reason or another. The other forms of treatment can still work for you. However, as I've suggested before, consider trying it.

Going on a Body Trip

Another part of self-treatment in Phase I without a partner is this: Enter the state of Erotic Focus in the way you have learned . . . and now, within your mind, go on a "body trip." In your relaxed E.F. float, set out to explore your body *within your mind*—without any physical touching or manipulation . . .

Think slowly and carefully about the different parts of your body and try to visualize them with eyes closed—*feel* the different areas, without actually touching them. Concentrate your thoughts on the external part of your genitals . . . the clitoris . . . the entrance to the vagina . . . the inside of your vagina . . . and try to get in touch vividly, *joining mind with body,* with the different sexual sensations available from all these different areas. The clarifying E.F. state helps significantly.

While you are doing all this in your mind, always regard your body in a totally "friendly" way. Don't be angry or resentful in any sense with what you may have regarded bitterly as "my anorgasmic body . . . my uncooperative body . . . my ugly body." Realize that it is not your body, *it is your mind that blocks the full physiological response.*

You can be confident that your body, having passed muster in a preceding thorough physical examination, has been certified as perfectly well equipped to experience orgasm. You must now learn to get back in touch with it. I assure you that many others have proved that by taking a "body trip," as you have been instructed here, you can help yourself to overcome your anorgasmia, as you fervently desire. *The doing is up to you.*

Masturbation as Self-Treatment

Before we go on to Phase II, it is easier and more productive first to experiment with the reflex response of orgasm through masturbation. *No pressure on you,* but before setting this method aside if the whole idea bothers you, consider the background first.

There is no question that most individuals explore themselves in childhood and adolescence, as well as in adulthood, before engaging in intercourse. They have experimented and learned the orgasmic response through masturbation. As with all sexual practices, masturbation is highly individual—approaches and manipulation differ from one person to another. The technique described here can serve as a guideline to test reactions of your own body *(only if you wish)* as part of overcoming your anorgasmia.

Step 1. First, enter the state of Erotic Focus, but without the usual arm levitation, until you are floating pleasantly, totally relaxed. Now focus your attention on your genitals. Proceed easily, at your own unpressured pace, gently rub your breasts . . . and then your clitoris (or simultaneously, one hand caressing one or both breasts, and the other hand manipulating your clitoris lightly, never roughly or too forcefully) . . .

Some women enjoy watching themselves masturbating, and you certainly may do so if you like. If you are not lubricated sufficiently, use a body lotion or light cream or gel of your choice. As you continue the manipulations, slowly and rhythmically, become acutely aware of the pleasurable sensations you are enjoying thoroughly . . .

Just allow yourself, while relaxed in your E.F. float, to explore your body and play with yourself until your bodily senses are so excited that *orgasm will just occur naturally*—no desperation, no duress, no forcing. Simply let the orgasm build and come to fruition.

Actually, once you have reached the critical level of physical arousal, *orgasm is just a reflex reaction of the involved muscles being in tension*. When you are anorgasmic, the problem is primarily that you don't let the involved muscles reach the peak of arousal required for the orgasm to occur.

Step 2. Now, as you climax, fully enjoy each moment of it and *register it in your brain!* This is extremely important—that you feel the orgasm *mentally* as well as physically; let the sensations penetrate and spread in every tingling way . . . on . . . and on . . .

Do not pull back, physically or emotionally. Don't feel at all embarrassed or guilty. Understand fully that this is a helpful *"learning experience"* for you. So let yourself be pleasured—the purpose is to assimilate and process the orgasm sensations fully in your brain.

As you recall from what you have read already in this book about basic sexuality, the brain is a vital part of the sexual experience, and, most probably, *the brain is the part that has been holding you back from reaching orgasm.* Please realize and accept that fact thoroughly.

Once your "brain computer" has registered the orgasmic reflex response, it will eventually—as you follow instructions here—respond quite automatically in the same way when you are with a partner. Now, after you know you *can* reach orgasm through masturbation, *you have proved an essential point to yourself.* Use the technique you have learned to emerge from the Erotic Focus state.

If you like, repeat the entire masturbation process when you choose to, as part of overcoming your anorgasmia. But again, if you simply cannot bring yourself to touch your body and to masturbate, don't force the issue. Use the other techniques of your own selection covered in this section to improve your sexual ease and enjoyment.

PHASE II—WITH A PARTNER

Having completed Phase I, you should already be comfortable with the sensation of orgasm by yourself . . . and you go on to the next stage of reaching your goal. *You will learn how to respond and reach orgasm with your partner.*

If you are in an ongoing relationship, in marriage or otherwise, open communication is strongly recommended. Discuss the matter candidly with your partner, in a relaxed and amicable fashion, never coming on in an overly emotional, antagonistic or accusing way. Nor should you be apologetic or subservient.

Simply, quietly explain calmly and frankly that you have a problem reaching orgasm, and that you wish to discuss how to overcome it together. Say forthrightly that you want and need his considerate cooperation. In a caring relationship, concurrence will certainly be forthcoming, along with gratitude for your honesty and trust.

Don't be embarrassed about discussing with him vital considerations such as foreplay, clitoral stimulation, or other actions that arouse you. *Your new self-confidence is based on knowing now how to be stimulated to reach orgasm.* Keep in mind, as pointed out, that timing is part of a successful result. Communicate fully and openly while having sex—tell him if you are coming to climax, whether you are close or right on the verge, or not yet near to orgasm.

If it is difficult for you to put these intimate details into direct words, then another way for you to progress is to guide him with your hand into the areas where you would like most to be stimulated. It's a big mistake, and one of the most common and destructive errors, to assume that he should know. (Think about it—do you really know *what he most wants you to do,* unless he tells you or guides you?)

In the event that he has ejaculated before you have had your orgasm, encourage him to stimulate you manually or orally or both, whatever you want, in order to pleasure you most. Silence is not golden here. It is damaging not only to you but to your entire relationship. If you don't reach orgasm, you probably will feel frustrated, whether you realize it or not. That leads to expressed or suppressed anger and resentment, detrimental to you both.

There is nothing wrong with coming to orgasm after him, *separately.* He will appreciate your telling him what to do, so that he can feel wonderful about giving you similar gratification. As cautioned earlier, if you fake having an orgasm, that is not a solution for you or for him, since it will intensify your basic orgasmic dysfunction and that will result in magnifying your problem as time goes on.

Using E.F. in Phase II

The first few times of communicating and experimenting openly, use the Erotic Focus exercise *shortly before engaging in sex,* not while having sex. By entering the E.F. float beforehand, your body will be physically relaxed, and your mind will be set to enjoy the sexual proceedings to the full.

While you are bringing on the E.F. float, just start thinking about your partner and what you enjoy about him . . . and then shift your awareness towards your genitals and let your mind dwell on them and on getting ready to be pleasured and to give pleasure . . . on beginning to lubricate . . . on getting engorged . . . aroused about having exciting, fulfilling interaction with your partner . . .

Now, in your E.F. float, with your mind free and yet in full control . . . join your partner, ready and loving throughout your mind and body. Go on naturally to mutual arousal and orgasm—forget about your state of Erotic Focus which has served its purpose here and will dissipate and disappear by itself.

If a "New" Relationship . . .

If the situation is other than marriage or a close relationship, perhaps with a *new* partner, you can proceed in one of two ways in respect to acting to overcome your anorgasmia:

1. Having tried and been conditioned, advancing through your self-treatment in Phase I, just go ahead . . . knowing that you have "taught" your body to respond, and that you will come to orgasm accordingly.

2. Tell your partner candidly and trustfully that you are a

bit apprehensive about sex . . . that in the past you have experienced some difficulties at times in coming to climax . . . but that you really want to be with him. Assure him that if you don't have an orgasm, he should not feel that it is a reflection on him. In addition, you should discuss with him openly and frankly how to pleasure each other maximally, a communication that is best for both of you.

In regard to using E.F. with a new partner, if you have the opportunity, you should take a few seconds beforehand to enter the state of Erotic Focus and then proceed as instructed earlier in Phase II. Otherwise, if the sexual joining occurs spontaneously, you might—as you go along—just let your mind move into the sensation of floating. This is not as helpful as actually going into E.F. but, since you are an expert in the E.F. technique by now, your body may just respond automatically.

11
COMBATING MALE IMPOTENCE: CORRECTING ERECTION PROBLEMS

The inability to obtain erection of the penis is generally referred to as erectile dysfunction. The condition can be due to *physical* (organic) or *psychological* factors.

What happens physiologically is that the body's "vascular reflex mechanism" fails to pump enough blood into the "cavernous sinuses" (channels) of the penis to make it firm and erect. The erectile and ejaculatory reflexes can be separate, so some impotent men who don't get an erection still can ejaculate even with a limp penis.

Difficulties in attaining and maintaining an erection are not uncommon and may occur at any age. It is generally reassuring and supportive to understand this fact: *Approximately half the male population has experienced occasional transient episodes of impotence.*

Such temporary, passing incidents are called *secondary* impotence. In contrast, *primary* impotence exists in men who have never been able to be potent with a partner, although they may have erections while masturbating, or have spontaneous erections in other situations.

It is encouraging to men who have occasional failures to become fully erect to understand that their "secondary impotence" can usually be treated with erectile function restored and continuing. On the other hand, "primary impotence" is frequently associated with serious underlying psychological problems which may require treatment with more conventional psychotherapy.

Our concern and goal here is to help correct and overcome *secondary* impotence, and to help remedy this quite common problem through pleasant, easily used self-treatment with the Erotic Focus technique. You'll find out exactly how E.F. has worked simply and effectively for many men.

First, it helps for you to understand the usual causes of impotence, both physical and psychological.

Common Physical Causes

Impotence may be brought on by a variety of physical causes, ranging from everyday stresses and demands to a number of disorders and diseases, including:

- fatigue, exhaustion, stress, anxiety, pressure, strain, shock
- diabetes
- chronic illnesses of any kind

- low hormonal level
- excessive use of drugs
- excessive use of alcohol
- taking various medications such as sleeping pills, tranquilizers, blood pressure pills, and a variety of other drugs
- neurological illnesses (involving nerves and nervous systems as related to the sex organs)
- prostatic conditions (involving the male prostate gland)
- venereal diseases (including Herpes)

In addition, *specific diseases* of the penis may be implicated. These will be detected by the physician in a thorough medical examination, which is a *must* in the event of impotence. Such disorders include: Peyronie's disease of the penis [of unknown origin, may involve pain during erections, often prevents intromission (insertion into the vagina)], Phimosis and Paraphimosis (disorders of the foreskin of the penis), Balanitis (inflammation of the tip of the penis), Squamus cell carcinoma (cancerous growth), venereal lesions, including syphilis, gonorrhea, herpes.

I must emphasize again that, at onset of impotence, fear of diseases and disorders of the penis (unlikely) should not spur anxiety and dread. Do have a medical checkup without delay if impotence continues.

Common Psychological Causes

Following a medical checkup, which probably will rule out *physical disease* as the cause of the impotence, try working with the program I recommend here. If the problem persists, consider consultation with a qualified professional, such as a psychiatrist, psychologist, or other qualified therapist. You will wish to consider carefully the following primary psychological causes of impotence, to check for yourself too whether one or more of these factors may be affecting you:

- fear, shame, or guilt about sexuality
- destructive interactions between a couple about sex
- anger and resentment in other areas between a couple
- control and power conflicts between a couple, in sex and/or otherwise
- castration anxiety—unconscious fear of being castrated or severely punished in some physical way for having sex

Self-Treatment with E.F.

Learning and using the Erotic Focus technique has helped many of my patients to correct and overcome common psychological causes of their sexual dysfunctions, with gratifying, enduring benefits.

As part of the self-treatment, I strongly recommend *open discussion* between the dysfunctional male and partner—wife, fiancée, girlfriend or male lover if dysfunction occurs in a homosexual relationship. Successful sex therapy is based on both partners understanding that *anxiety occurring at the moment of sexual intercourse can disrupt the male's ability to have an erection.* One of the main objectives of effective therapy therefore is to banish this anxiety and to adopt an optimistic attitude about treatment, in order to help correct the impotence and prevent recurrence.

It's therefore vital to clarify and agree on *no-pressure* sexual attitudes. It's essential to create and continue a relaxed, mutually comforting setting, building assurance that the impotence problem will be corrected.

Many of my patients have restored sexual ease and confidence with the aid of the Erotic Focus method. Again, frank, friendly, nonbelligerent, loving exchanges between both partners can be a great aid in speeding the wanted restorative results through E.F.

E.F. Self-Treatment Strategy

The initial E.F. self-treatment strategy is twofold:

1. To utilize effectively *the personal stimulation factors which you possess,* that is, to arouse sexually through manipulation with hands, lips, mouth and tongue (as well as with the penis), all part of your physical sexual potential.

2. To decrease and eventually to gain dominance over those factors which create *certain negative sexual anxi-*

ety effects. Such elements form the basis of the inability to attain and maintain penis erection during intercourse. Effective treatment aims to attain control over these negatives and eliminate them.

Here are the clear, simple instructions to follow:

FIRST STAGE OF SELF-TREATMENT

Every day perform the E.F. exercise which you have learned, approximately three times *by yourself.* When you have entered the state of Erotic Focus, concentrate in your mind on visualizing very clearly a flat white surface such as a movie or TV screen, on which a picture is to be beamed and then viewed by you alone.

Now, on this screen, I want you to *project your personal sexual fears,* as if you are operating a videocassette which you have recorded. In your mind, imagine one of your typical sexual episodes in which you have erection problems.

When you look at and examine these re-created actual happenings on the screen, allow your feelings to surface inside of you and try to become fully aware of *what triggers your fears and anxieties,* the probable basic causes of your sexual dysfunctioning. As an aid, check this listing:

Typical Fears and Anxieties

Here are the dominant *fears* experienced and expressed by my sexually dysfunctioning male patients (compare with your own):

1. *Fear of having no erection at all,* feeling very embarrassed about the inability to erect . . . and becoming increasingly incapable in this function.

2. *Fear of being laughed at* or seeming weak and ridiculous to your partner.

3. *Fear of being harshly criticized* and demeaned by the partner, silently or aloud.

4. *Fear of starting with a semi-hard erection* and of losing it at the moment of entry (once that failing has been experienced previously).

5. *Fear of losing the erection* during sexual intercourse, and thus causing your sexual partner to feel rejected, unloved, unattractive, frustrated, angry.

In addition to specific fears, male dysfunctioning can also be brought on by *anxieties*. Here's a checklist of the most common anxieties:

1. *Anxiety over losing the highly valued, supportive love* of the partner, and the enduring, boundless quality of that affection.

2. *Anxiety over losing the bolstering, ego-building respect* of the partner.

3. *Anxiety over losing your own self-esteem* as a total, well-functioning individual.

4. *Anxiety over never again being capable* of having sexual intercourse with this or any other partner.

5. *Pervading anxieties* about the partner's rejection and possible leaving . . . and of the partner getting involved with someone else, thus triggering added destructive feelings of envy and jealousy.

6. *Anxiety about one's own complete masculinity;* typical thought: "I'm no longer a man who can perform."

7. *Anxiety that the partner will not be patient* and will not wait until the problem has been solved, leading to the despairing thought that it may never be solved.

8. *Anxiety about possible latent homosexuality* which may

mean that "I'm a homosexual and don't even know it—can I live with that?"

Now, having absorbed carefully the preceding list of some of the most common *fears* and *anxieties* which afflict many individuals with erectile dysfunction, take as much time as necessary to *pinpoint your own primary apprehension*. Think it through—the rewards can be tremendous. Review your inner alarms and stresses along lines like these:

Is your principal fear or anxiety one of those listed in the preceding? Is it something else that you haven't really comprehended up to now? Take time to think it through.

If the precise cause is not clear to you yet, wait a while . . . and then enter the Erotic Focus state again. The picture will come into focus most clearly and definitively if you enter E.F. repeatedly. Soon you will gain a *thorough understanding of what is your own primary fear or anxiety*.

This stage should cover four or more days, depending on one's individual application and progress. At this point, after realizing just what triggers your dysfunctioning, you can proceed in one of two ways . . .

1. *Discuss the entire problem* with your partner openly and frankly, as you have clarified it for yourself. Introduce the subject quietly and calmly. Invite understanding, input and cooperation from your partner. You might both learn that the problem is related to *something she does or doesn't do*—or to some action or misdirection in approach and procedure *on your part*.

This mind-expanding course can improve your relationship wonderfully. It can open the door to greatly enhanced mutual physical and emotional rewards never achieved by the two of you before. I recommend this strategy strongly.

2. *If you prefer not to discuss* the whole situation at this point, revealing your new findings and revelations to your partner, then you must concentrate, with the clarifying aid of E.F., to put the problem into the right perspective for yourself.

Repeat the Erotic Focus exercise whenever you can find a few moments of privacy at any time of the day or night. *Things that were fuzzy will come into focus.* Usually, once you are able to visualize and understand your condition, you can discuss it openly with your partner. Thus, it is likely to clear up gradually, and you can function again as desired.

After you enter the Erotic Focus state—before any and all the stages of E.F. self-treatment—as explained in detail in the following pages, do not be concerned about emerging from E.F. Your Erotic Focus float will dissipate naturally by itself during the periods of sexual play, and later during and after intercourse.

Now you proceed with your partner to the second phase of your remedial treatment.

SECOND STAGE OF SELF-TREATMENT

My recommendations for self-treatment parallel to some extent routines described by Masters and Johnson. Similar techniques are used effectively by many qualified sex therapists in their treatment approaches. *My Erotic Focus method adds a great deal to the fundamental procedures*—to bring about desired beneficial results quickly and enduringly in the self-treatment instructed here.

For five to seven days of this second stage of remedial treatment (the length of time depends on when you feel ready for the third stage), you and your partner are to proceed with lovemaking, enjoying sexual intimacy. However, *you will refrain from actual intercourse, from insertion of the penis into the vagina, and from ejaculation, whether due to vaginal or oral stimulation.*

Each night and/or morning, or any time of day or night that you both prefer—depending on when you usually like to have sex—you are to do the following:

First, you, the male, go into the Erotic Focus state which you have learned, but your partner does not enter E.F. at this point. While you are in E.F., your partner is to caress you with her hands and mouth all over your body—*but not in your genital area.* While you are in E.F., your senses are heightened and you will experience your partner's caresses with the fullest enjoyment, *short of ejaculation.*

If you find yourself on the verge of ejaculating, ask her to ease up. If your partner finds herself about to have an orgasm, she should permit herself to come, *but she should continue caressing you during and after her orgasm.*

Her caressing should go on for about five to ten minutes. Then you bring yourself out of the Erotic Focus state, using the technique you've learned, or simply let the float dissipate . . .

Now you are to *tell your partner in detail* how her caresses felt on your body . . . and, of prime importance, exactly what she did to you that you enjoyed the most, that is, where she touched you . . . when . . . how.

Second, now it is *your turn* to take over the active caressing, pleasuring phase of treatment. Ask your partner to go into the Erotic Focus state, or, if she prefers not to enter E.F., she is to relax thoroughly, to anticipate your attentions, and become ready to be caressed in turn . . .

In this step, you do not enter E.F. When she says she is ready for your pleasuring, you will caress her with your hands and mouth—all over her body—*but not caressing or kissing her genital area.* Touch and fondle her face, arms, breasts, back, buttocks, abdomen, legs— gently, lovingly, never roughly. Register in full, with your alert, enlivened senses, how her skin feels in all the different places of her body—except for the genital area . . .

If you find yourself on the verge of ejaculating, ease up a little until you are in control again. If your partner finds herself on the verge of having an orgasm, she should let herself go, and you should *continue* with pleasuring her—*but not in the genital area*—during and after her orgasm, even if she goes on into further orgasms . . .

This mutual, turnabout pleasuring—first female caressing male, then male pleasuring the female—is to be repeated for two to three nights and/or mornings, longer if you both deem it necessary. Continue until both partners feel fully satisfied and totally anxiety-free while participating in and enjoying the lovemaking periods.

You may well have had spontaneous erections while you were caressing and pleasuring each other, but go right on—although letting up if you are about to ejaculate. Such spontaneous erections should be enjoyed, *but do not allow yourself to ejaculate.*

THIRD STAGE OF SELF-TREATMENT

Now that you have both arrived at the essential point where you are both enjoying the pleasurable caressing and are free of anxiety in this preliminary period of making love, *you are both to caress and to pleasure each other at the same time*—in the same way as followed while taking turns before.

However, first, before you begin the pleasuring period, both of you are to take about 20 seconds to go into E.F., in order to be fully relaxed and in full contact with your heightened senses. Then, with each caressing the other at the same time, *you are both still avoiding touching the genital areas, with fingers or orally*. Much as you both enjoy the sensations, *you are not to permit yourself (the male) to come to ejaculation,* no matter how many times your partner comes to orgasm.

It is vital that you continue each step for the extended periods noted in the instructions, two to three days for this stage. This provides enough time to assimilate and process in your mind the different sensations and lessons you are deriving from each stage. Rushing the process and treatments tends to not reduce performance anxiety sufficiently—and would limit and even retard the wanted and needed beneficial and restorative developments.

FOURTH STAGE OF SELF-TREATMENT

This stage is similar to the second stage of the treatment—to the first procedure where your partner caresses you, but with this vital difference: *Now she touches and caresses your genitals with her hands and orally,* as well as all over your body as before.

You may get erections, partially or fully, in this phase. If so, just allow your mind to register the pleasant sensations of your erecting penis. If it then should become soft and limp, and go flaccid again, don't become upset . . . just drift and wait for a bit . . . take a few breaths, and concentrate on Erotic Focus floating.

Then your partner should begin to caress your penis again, and she should kiss it tenderly, lovingly, continuing the entire interaction for five or ten minutes, the same as in the earlier stage, except that she is now including your genital area specifically. Important reminder now, as before: *You are not to ejaculate under any circumstances.*

After this phase has proceeded for the recommended period, it is your turn, as before, to pleasure your partner, *now including manual and oral touching of her genitals.* As noted, you must not permit yourself to ejaculate, but if she gets very excited during the time you are touching her, it is fine for her to come to orgasm, and perhaps repeatedly as you go on caressing her.

However, no matter how excited you and she become, *do not insert your penis in her, even if you have a strong erection.*

Next, you caress and you pleasure each other *simultaneously.* No matter how worked up you may become, don't allow yourself to ejaculate. It is vital for successful treatment and the enduring result you want that you gradually grow 100 percent confident by going through all the preceding stages exactly as instructed. This stage should be carried through for two to three nights and/or mornings, or longer if you feel it's desirable.

Now, having both become experts at giving pleasure to each other you have advanced to enjoying the interaction *without inserting your penis and having ejaculations yourself,* although your partner has had that freedom. Up to this point, it usually takes an average of six to ten days for the male with erectile dysfunction to become fully ready to go on to attaining and maintaining successful erection and intercourse.

FIFTH, CONCLUDING STAGE OF SELF-TREATMENT

After full confidence in pleasuring and erectile ability has been established, intercourse is resumed between you and your partner. Here is the strategy you are to follow for achieving enduring success:

1. Lie on your back and go into the state of Erotic Focus.

Now your partner and you are to caress and stimulate each other manually and orally as you both personally like best until you have an erection, as you have both practiced and accomplished.

When your erection is firm, your partner is to sit on top of you, lowering herself on to your penis which will slide into her vagina.

Then she is to move up and down rhythmically and rather quickly, retaining your penis in her vagina. You are not to move your penis, just focus on the pleasurable sensations you are getting from your partner's movements . . . up . . . down . . . up . . . down . . .

Still, do not let her stimulate you fully to orgasm at this point, but separate gently *before* you come to ejaculation (it is important to refrain from actual ejaculation now in order to erase any feeling whatsoever that you may be "performing"). You should not miss any of the marvelous variety of sexual pleasure all along the way in lovemaking; realize that the orgasm is not the only significant or ultimate, lasting effect.

2. Begin again in the same way as in the phase just explained—you on your back, with your partner sitting on you and your penis within her—but this time *you* become active and thrust your penis in and out of your partner's vagina in rhythm with her . . .

Now let your penis be stimulated fully to orgasm—your objective all along—*wunderbar!*

Don't consider these two phases in this position—your partner sitting on you and moving up and down on your penis, then you thrusting your penis in and up and down in rhythm—to be the only and permanent positions of intercourse. They are gratifying in themselves but are a transition to the essential goal which is: *Secure and confident sexual activities in whatever positions and experiments you desire, but always in a nondemanding no-pressure, anxiety-free mood and environment.*

The two-step strategy explained in this fifth stage generally should take two to four nights and/or mornings until your confidence is built up and solidly established. Moreover, now when regular sexual activities are resumed, as in the period before any erection problems developed, you and your partner should make it a natural, rewarding part of your living.

Be sure to keep the newly learned channels of communication, mutual giving and accepting participation open. This is essential in order not to fall back into the previous, destructive, anxiety-producing patterns. Enjoy sex at your own pace, as pleases you both the most; you are not in a race nor trying to score or break any records. *Pleasure yourselves in your own personal preferred ways and at your own chosen times and frequency.*

If there is a relapse of impotence (unlikely to occur if you continue to communicate and cooperate as taught here), you and your partner should go back either to the entire sequence of treatment stages, or at least to the last two steps, as instructed.

You may continue or resume the Erotic Focus exercise prior to intercourse as long as necessary and desired, as always helpful and enjoyable. The choice differs with each person, according to the individual's needs. One who has difficulty "unwinding," in general, will probably benefit from doing the E.F. technique every time his business or other problems and anxieties are on his mind.

Always be aware of the importance and even necessity for getting into "neutral gear," relaxed and unburdened, in order to enjoy sex freely and fully. Your E.F. technique will work for you dependably. As long as you use it, you can count on this revivifying method for relaxation.

Self-Treatment in a ''New'' Relationship

In the first sexual occasion in a new relationship, or a casual contact, it is advisable to handle the situation this way:

Take a chance and go right ahead with the sexual proceedings as though nothing is wrong and you have no concern. Then, if the dysfunction appears, and you cannot have an erection, begin a discussion about your problem in a relaxed way. Don't pass it off as not happening, or make empty excuses about it. If you try to ignore it completely, you will only set the stage for fear and uncertainty in future encounters.

That course will make you even more anxious the next time you are with someone sexually. Also, it's likely to make your partner feel badly, troubled that it is her/his fault, that lack of sexual attractiveness or feeling or know-how has caused your impotence on this occasion.

If you cannot bring yourself to speak up, if instead you mumble an excuse, that ''this has never happened before''. . . or that ''I haven't been well''. . . then nothing is resolved. As a general rule, I strongly advise from professional experience that *it is better to clear the air.* It will take much pressure off you about suppressing awareness of your dysfunction, and it will help avoid frustration in both partners.

You can cover the matter in a very simple way, such as, ''Please understand that I'm very attracted to you. I want very much to make love to you. However, I'm afraid that, at times, I get so excited mentally that I lose my erection physically. If that happens, please be patient and don't take it personally. It's my problem, not yours. If I don't get or hold the erection, we'll just have to find another way of pleasuring each other.''

Remember, don't be afraid to speak up. Most people will be more sensitive and caring than you may think in this situation.

12 MAXIMUM SEXUAL FULFILLMENT LIFELONG

Happy sexual activity is basically the extension of active living and maintaining a positive interest. Right now, and through all your years ahead, you can enjoy and extend your sexual pleasure to your maximum personal capacity and desires, with your Erotic Focus exercises.

My advice and recommendations for better sex are applicable lifelong. As I emphasize repeatedly, E.F. will work for you if you work with it. That's up to *you*, whether you're in your late teens or older, decade after decade, into your fifties, sixties, seventies.

Enjoying all aspects of sexual activity is basically not an age but an attitude: You must maintain to the full a continuing outlook of awareness and striving for new discovery and deeper insights. That means using your potentials to the fullest extent of your abilities—mental, emotional, and physical. Add to that the informed understanding at any age that gratifying sexual intercourse is not a matter of how often, but how loving.

Impetuous "hurry-up" sex—usually youthful rather than mature—centers specifically on reaching explosive orgasm. With experience, the focus is more likely to be on slower, caring lovemaking. This aspect might well be compared to the difference between gulping a fast-foods hamburger versus dining appreciatively and knowledgeably on a magnificent, expertly created gourmet meal. Age is no barrier in either case.

For better sex, I suggest that you ask yourself: "Do I concern myself too much about how often I have sex . . . or am I aware always of how much mutual, sharing pleasure my partner and I gain, how much *closeness* we both derive?" It is worth your reflecting on the comment of a mature friend: "In later years, as I treasure each moment of living more, I feel that *there just isn't time to rush sexual intercourse.* Each detail of enjoyment is too valuable to waste."

Human beings slow down sexually to some degree naturally, of course, with passing time. You can't run as fast as in earlier years, either, nor should you try to. Take your cue from the story of the small boy whose knees, shins, elbows and hands were constantly bruised from falling down.

"Why do you fall down so much?" a neighbor asked.

"Because," he explained logically, "I try to run faster than I can run."

We vary considerably as individuals in our desires and capacities in all areas, at any time. Some people pursue sex enthusiastically and inventively way beyond the average. In general, though, most individuals and couples experience and accept naturally a normal decline in sexual desire over the life cycle. It's certainly nothing to worry about unless abrupt changes are involved.

There is overall professional consensus that the sex drive and desire is stronger in very young men, then gradually diminishes. In contrast, women as a whole tend to have a slightly lower drive and desire at the outset of their sexual lives—with an added peak of desire in their thirties and forties, then a gradual decline. Finally their sex drive tends to match that of males in later years.

Keep in mind, however, that you are an *individual,* not a generalization. Be guided by your *personal* wants and needs at any age. Even if you lose some vigor in "making sex," through the years you probably have developed a more thoughtful, more feeling, more mature ability to *make love.*

It's heartening to appreciate this universal truth: Fullest enjoyment of sex is not primarily a *physical reaction* but—far more life-nourishing—it's an *emotional uplift* of enduring sustenance. A wise elderly woman told me, "What I have always found more important in sex is not the go-go-go of hectic intercourse, but the loving *afterglow.* That will never cease for my husband and me—no matter how long we live."

By using the E.F. float, instructed in detail later in this chapter, you can help remove destructive blocks based on misinformation and anxieties. These, unfortunately, rank high among some people, especially as they mature. Such misconceptions may affect their sexual interest and participation negatively—*unnecessarily.*

In a typical instance, I clarified the facts to a very intelligent male patient, Cleve, who was concerned about his masculinity. He said thoughtfully, "I see. It's not just the extent of the erection. It's the extension of what a man and woman have learned during years of shared experience and intimacy. It's the culmination of everything that has contributed to our enduring partnership and l-o-v-e.''

I smiled, ''I couldn't have said it better myself. I'm going to use that in my book.'' And now I have.

Counteracting Diminished Sexual Interest

This practicable, step-by-step example of how lessened interest and participation in sex can be remedied is typical of cases I have seen in my office (and as experienced by many other professionals) innumerable times. Think how the considerations here can be specifically helpful at any age—perhaps for you—certainly for some individuals you care about very much.

An attractive fifty-six-year-old woman, Jenny, had been married, divorced, then later married again. She had three grown children, and had been with her second husband, Eliot, for twenty-one years when she came to see me. She and her husband worked together in a thriving retail fashion business. She was exceptionally well dressed, with an air of executive competence.

She provided further proof that appearances can be very deceptive, for her seeming self-confidence was on the surface only. After a few minutes of conversation, she took a deep breath, ''I'm here because for the past four years I've lost interest in sex.'' She shrugged listlessly. ''I figure it's a matter of aging—after all, I'm well past fifty. But a close friend said, 'You're too young to die sexually.' She insisted that I see you.''

It developed that ''For the first fifteen years of our marriage, Eliot and I were very good together sexually. I enjoyed sex far more than in my first marriage, which was pretty dull. Orgasms? Terrific! Then I began to back off due to pain during intercourse . . .''

I asked, ''Did the pain continue and keep you from sex?''

''Well, yes,'' she continued. ''A number of times, we tried intercourse, with his penis in me, but I couldn't enjoy it at all—it hurt. Eliot was becoming more and more upset. Finally I went to see my gynecologist for the first time in years. He found some problems, and as a result . . . I had a hysterectomy, but . . .'' She sighed hopelessly.

''Has it been better since the hysterectomy?''

''The pain disappeared,'' she went on, ''but so did my interest in sex. If anything, things became worse. I tried to avoid any intimacy. When we went to bed at night, I'd linger in the bathroom a long time, hoping Eliot would fall asleep meanwhile. Or, in bed, if he started to touch me, I'd pretend I was asleep . . .'' She sighed, ''Well, you can imagine, things went from bad to worse. The crux of it is—I'm just too *old!*''

''How did your husband react to all this?'' I nudged.

''Terrible. He took my lack of response as a personal rejection. I just couldn't explain . . . I kept making excuses. We had frequent arguments, then we wouldn't talk to each other for days. Out of frustration, he started overeating—and how. The poor guy, he has put on over eighty pounds in the past four years—he's close to three hundred pounds now, a real mess . . .''

"How did his overweight affect you?"

She frowned, shaking her head. "What do you think? The heavier he became, the more repulsive I found him. Sex? Forget it!" She shivered helplessly. "I know it's really my fault. I'm so depressed, I can't see any way out. Neither of us wants a divorce—we really love each other underneath, but we just can't cope with our problems. Getting old is terrible!"

First Stage of Treatment

To relieve her considerable distress as we talked, I guided her into the state of Erotic Focus. As she relaxed deeply, yet was thoroughly alert and mentally focused, I assured her that neither "aging" nor the pain and subsequent surgery were at the base of her sexual lack of interest. She was listening intently, without strain.

I explained, "You should understand this, that *sex* is a natural function of your body. That's just as true now for you as in past years. For most of your life, you let your body respond naturally to sexual thoughts and feelings and reactions. And apparently you enjoyed sex thoroughly—is that right?"

With a glimmer of a smile, she nodded her agreement, thinking, recalling past pleasures.

"But," I went on, "for about the past four years, since your vaginal pain—and then after the hysterectomy—*you curbed your natural responses*. Do you realize that clearly?"

"I suppose so," she said, eyes wide open and aware. "Yes."

"In that way," I noted, "you developed what is

called an 'avoidance mechanism' which *blocks your sexual desire.*"

"I see . . ."

"Good." I smiled. "Here's what I want you to do now: Simply relax your body physically every evening before going to bed. Don't think at all about sex. Just go into the state of Erotic Focus to register how relaxed and yet aware your body feels, how light and free you feel all over . . ."

We went over the E.F. technique several times together until it became very easy and natural for her to feel the relaxed state of buoyant floating sensation. Also, I discussed with her many of the highlights about sexuality that are covered in detail throughout this book. Much of this was all new and very enlightening to her as it is for most people, although they've never admitted it to themselves or others.

Second Stage of Consultation

When she returned for her second visit, she reported excellent progress. "E.F. gave me a sense of freedom and openness." She said that a few days after our session, she began to discuss with her husband her lack of interest in intercourse in recent years, and then the problems of his overweight. "Before," she stated, "I avoided sex but never told him why. And I never mentioned his overweight. His reaction was remarkably understanding."

She was able to tell Eliot that she had come to me for help, and that I had suggested discussion without her previous fear that he'd be angry. She smiled, "Eliot reassured me that he would do everything he could to help me. Our talks cleared the air. It was wonderful—we had intercourse several times, with marvelous orgasms such as I hadn't enjoyed in years." She laughed, "At my age—when I thought my sex life was over!"

She explained her routine. "As you advised, every night I'd lie down in bed and go into my E.F. float as you instructed. I could actually feel my body release the tension built up during the day. While in E.F., I'd go over your instructions—that sex is a natural function of the body at any age, that by squelching interest, I was depriving myself of pleasurable sensations."

Recalling, she went on, "I remembered your words—*'Sex communicates love and affection'*. I realized keenly that I was depriving our relationship of this important tool of communication. Thinking in those terms, my body became alive and aroused, and I was quite fully responsive to Eliot's advances. It's like a miracle—how our love and lovemaking have revived and are better than ever"—she giggled like a schoolgirl—"at our age!"

Final Stage of Understanding

On her third and last visit, she said that she had shared the detailed information about sex with Eliot, and that they talked about it frankly, as never before. "Then," she stated, "I taught him the E.F. technique, and with its help we've come to a wonderful new understanding about our relationship."

She said that she'd spilled out to her husband a lot of anger and resentment she'd accumulated through their "cold war years," aside from sex. She told him that he'd never given her enough credit for her good ideas which had helped build their business. Her bitterness had expanded and festered within her when they went to bed. "I felt like a prostitute having to make love with so much anger inside me. Eliot was astounded. He had no idea I felt like that, and said he very much appreciated all my contributions to the business and at home. He also told me he loved me, something he hadn't said in a long time."

It became clear now that, coupled with her internal rage due to lack of recognition and praise, she had used her symptoms—due to her vaginal pain and then her concern about the hysterectomy—to retaliate by rejecting sex with her husband. "Now all that's on its way to being straightened out," she concluded. "It looks like fair sailing ahead, with E.F. helping us to keep our feelings relaxed and in focus."

As a further development in this case, Eliot arranged to consult with me about his overweight which, obviously, was tied in with negative feelings due to being rejected sexually by his wife. With the help of the Erotic Focus method and proper dieting, he was finally able to take off his excess weight. This proved a further aid in bolstering their total relationship, along with improving their enjoyment of sex.

Summary of E.F. Functions in this Case

Consider how these four Erotic Focus steps worked so well for Jenny and Eliot in their circumstances, and how they can provide helpful guidance for you at any time:

Step 1: Relax effectively with the Erotic Focus method—quickly, simply, enjoyably—as Jenny did.

Step 2: While in the E.F. state, use your focused concentration to analyze the situation clearly. Note, for instance, how Jenny came to understand that her symptoms (vaginal concerns) were linked to a lack of mature communication with her husband in other areas of their life together, not just the sexual aspects.

Step 3: Again use the E.F. state to strip away self-camouflage, and to penetrate previously hidden insights. Using Jenny as an example again, think of how she finally realized that she had been basically insecure, and therefore became fearful of losing her husband if she took a chance and spoke out frankly and openly. Out of this deeply imbedded fear, she hadn't spoken up for years in sexual and other aspects of their personal relationship—in this case, business involvement—and the result was resentment and anger.

Step 4: Review the lessons learned in the first three steps to gain greater control of your feelings, to assert your valid opinions and desires for communication and resultant security and supportive self-respect. Pilot yourself along the lines that helped Jenny immensely in her life-wrecking dilemma.

Whatever your situation, you can use these four fundamental steps repeatedly to attain better sex and happier living from now on.

Sexual Problems Due to Pain and Illness

Sexual enjoyment tends to diminish and even disappear in many instances when the pain and multiple pressures of physical or emotional illness afflict a person. This inevitably affects a couple in respect to sexual intercourse. The oppressive problems generally increase with time. Fortunately much relief is obtainable through self-treatment—and, of course, through added professional therapy in some cases.

All these facets of approach are essential:

1. Understanding the situation
2. Having a very strong desire to make things better
3. Then doing something positive and productive about it.

It's vital for all concerned to realize that effective remedial measures can be taken, and that the right approaches and follow-through will usually produce beneficial and even restorative results. Greater pleasure, comfort, mutual joy can be obtained, even in the most severe examples.

Here's another demonstration of how one can proceed to rectify sexual problems brought on by illness and pain. Each person's circumstances vary, of course, but the steps are similar. In the following instance, I suggest you spotlight all the details which you can use if the need exists, or might arise in the future and involve yourself or anyone close to you.

Lucy and Rick, both in their late forties, called on me for help in order to try to avoid an impending divorce crisis. Suddenly, after over twenty years of "very happy" marriage, Lucy had turned away from her husband physically, and had banned any further sexual intercourse.

"But I love Lucy more than ever," Rick insisted, "and I'm sure she loves me. This whole situation is crazy."

Tight-lipped, Lucy responded, "Certainly I love you. But you can get your sexual release somewhere else, from somebody else. Just don't tell me about it. I'm through with sex—it would kill me, and you know it!"

I learned bit by bit that Lucy had been in great pain, and finally had gone through long, complicated surgery in the vaginal area a year before. Now, although her doctors said that she was completely healed, and ready to resume normal sexual intercourse, she would have none of it.

Close to tears, she explained, "I went through so much physical pain and mental anguish, I'm not taking any chances of more such terrible suffering in my body and mind. Even to think about Rick's penis entering me makes me throb in agony."

"What she's really afraid of," Rick interjected, "is cancer. That's what killed her mother, and she's gotten it into her head that any further sexual intercourse will bring on fatal cancer for her. I just can't convince her otherwise . . ."

Fear, panic, foreboding—call it what you will—all

may be triggered by chronic pain and illness. This can occur at any time, but chances for onset appear to multiply considerably with added years. The course I recommended for this couple can probably be applied correctively by you or anyone you're concerned about under comparable situations . . .

Program for Similar Conditions

Step 1: To help provide immediate relief for both from their painful stress, I taught the Erotic Focus method to Lucy and Rick. They took to the technique very quickly, although neither was in the high range of E.F. potential. In their favor, both were highly motivated by intense desire for a solution to their crisis situation.

I suggested that they go into E.F. frequently each day, up to ten times for brief periods. I recommended further that whenever convenient they should go into the F.F. float at the same time. This, I underscored, would add another measure of cooperation and closeness which I felt was so essential in their partnership now. At this stage, during E.F., they were just to concentrate on floating along peacefully, feeling unburdened, at rest, secure.

Step 2: Lucy agreed to see her gynecologist within the week, after I spoke with him and explained the situation. He was most cooperative, eager to be helpful. He checked her condition thoroughly, then assured her emphatically that their sexual intercourse would have nothing to do with bringing on cancer. Furthermore, as repeated assurance, an arrangement was made for frequent checkups.

Step 3: In Lucy's follow-up visit with me, I pointed out how unreasonable it would be for her to refuse sexual intercourse and reject her husband, since it had been established medically that no physical harm or danger were involved. She seemed much more at ease, and nodded her understanding and relief. She commented that her E.F. sessions were helping her to relax and feel more at peace with herself and the world about her.

Unfortunately, a good many people fear that sexual involvement may aggravate chronic ills. Heart troubles, high blood pressure, asthma, emphysema, bronchial disorders—all are common afflictions that induce concern about sexual activity, but they're usually overrated.

If you, or anyone with whom you are involved, have any such sexual reluctance or fear, there is one sure way to resolve the matter: *have a thorough checkup, in which you ask specifically for advice about the effect of sexual exertions*. Then gauge your future sexual pursuits accordingly. Chances are you'll get a green light to indulge in sexual activity more than you had anticipated.

Step 4: I instructed Lucy about using the Erotic Focus method when making love with her husband—to help free herself from fear, and to allow *gradual penis penetration*, which she had negated because of earlier pain and dread of cancer.

Step 5: I encouraged Lucy to go alone into the state of E.F., and to focus on employing and enjoying sexual fantasies about making love—in order to help loosen her inhibitions further.

Step 6: As an adjunct, to improve her physical conditioning for better sex, I taught Lucy the simple *sexual exercises* which would strengthen her involved muscles for greater participation and pleasure for both her and her husband. Feeling more positive rather than negative about herself now, she took to the exercises readily and said she looked forward to performing them regularly. She added that she was going to sign up for general physical exercise classes, after I assured her that I knew women into their eighties who were benefiting from such proper conditioning.

Result: The corrective program described here usually overcomes average problems within two to six weeks. Lucy and Rick reported to me happily that they were back to their normal state of sexual enjoyment in less than a month. Both also wanted to continue their daily E.F. floats, individually and together, because the simple technique provided so much pleasurable relief from negative stress.

I must emphasize that more serious situations may require a longer time for normalization, and possibly additional psychotherapy, due to more ingrained and more complex problems.

A Real Plus: Sexual Exercises

One way of helping *yourself*—whether male or female—to stay sexually active and enjoying it thoroughly through the years is with regular sexual exercising, as instructed earlier. I suggest that you add to the sexual exercises a good body conditioning program, either by yourself at home or in classes. Brisk walking, swimming and bicycling are normally helpful at any age. But avoid overstraining yourself either with sexual or other exercises. Your guideline always should be: *If it hurts, stop!*

It's my experience with patients and others that keeping active sexually and otherwise helps one to keep "young" in sex, at any time, in spirit, and in body. An example is a dashing, energetic gentleman in his late seventies who asserted with a grin, "I'm not a dirty old man . . . I'm a sexy senior citizen."

A further tip about sexual exercises: If you are in your twenties or thirties, woman or man, my advice is that you do not delay until you are forty or older to commence and continue your sexual exercises regularly. The earlier you start in your adult years, the sooner you get the total and enduring benefits.

My recommendation to you at any age is that you aim to participate in sexual activity, in loving, in every positive aspect of daily living. Good health is certainly a factor, but, as you have noted in the illustrative preceding case histories, even illness and pain can be comforted and alleviated to a worthwhile degree by intelligent understanding and a loving sexual partnership. You *try* to make things better—to the fullest extent possible.

It is our combined, experienced conviction and recommendation to you that *nobody is ever too old for intimacy, sexual or otherwise.* Some of the greatest boons in life stem from giving, accepting, and sharing in a loving relationship.

13 The Most-Asked Questions About Sex—Answered

As a psychiatrist, I am often asked questions about sex. To supplement the information throughout this book, and to help you most, here are concise answers to many of the question asked of me and of other therapists I have checked. I have divided the questions into categories and indicated the source—man or woman—of the question. The answers are of value to both women and men, although they're usually asked by one or the other. The practicable solutions will probably apply to you too sooner or later.

Consider the answers also in regard to the problems of a partner or friend or relative. You may be able to assist them in finding possible solutions to a worrisome sexual dilemma. Furthermore, insights disclosed about one problem may often help you with other related hang-ups—without you having realized it before.

Making the Sexual Focus Method Work Best for You

I'm sure that by now you have learned and practiced the Erotic Focus technique well and are getting the wanted benefits already. The individual problems presented in this chapter, as well as on other pages, along with the practical answers, provide further excellent opportunity to refine exactly how you can tune in to your own problems and get the answers you need through E.F.

As brush-up practice, go into the E.F. float, and focus on the sexual situation where you wish to improve, or on a problem you want to solve. You, and you alone, now set up the "TV scene" portraying the circumstances for examining on your inner mental screen. Project the picture involving your concern, such as discerning the most effective way to communicate with and caress a desired partner in order to help you both to most enjoyable and fulfilling orgasms.

Now, in your E.F. concentrated awareness, "tune" the picture into sharp detail, and zoom in on discovering your best procedure. Try this tuning-in process repeatedly with a variety of pictures to see how effectively it works. You'll find that increasingly you'll be able, as Thoreau put it, *"to see beyond the range of sight."*

Sexual Desire

Yelling out sexually (man): "When I come, I want to yell out my excitement and joy, just let go completely. But my wife is silent even when she climaxes. I'm afraid she'd be disgusted if I roar out my passion. Do you have any advice about how we can both get to let go fully?"

Most people make some noises when coming—grunting, moaning, yelling, sighing, even crying. If your wife doesn't give one "peep," first ask her *if* she's really coming (maybe she's not). She's your partner—trust each other! If she says she *does* climax, then she may have conditioned herself to be silent, suppressing any vocal expression. This becomes a conditioned reflex, often due to fear that children or parents or others in adjacent rooms may hear.

If there's no need now to be concerned about people listening, then point out that letting go vocally is a natural, thrilling release for both. Ask her *what* makes her hold back, and whether that still makes sense. If it's a learned and conditioned reflex, encourage her now to "rehearse" having intercourse while in E.F., watching herself cry out on her inner screen, just to test her reactions.

Then, suggest this game of *exchanging roles:* She is to play *you,* and you will play *her*—that is, you'll be dead-silent during intercourse and orgasm (try, anyhow) and she's to yell and scream. And exchanging not only roles but feelings and fears about "letting go," you'll both learn a lot more about each other, deepening your love and sexual enjoyment. You may find a middle ground of expression—as both reach new heights of passion with exuberance. Are you both game to try?

Orgasm during sleep (woman): "I sometimes have trouble reaching orgasm during sex with my husband. Other times, I wake up from a sexy dream having a terrific orgasm. I'd rather have it during sex with my husband. How can I manage the shift?"

If you reach orgasm some of the time but not all the time, this may mean that you don't communicate well with your partner about sexual matters. Your partner cannot read your thoughts. *Tell* him what "turns you on" best to help you climax. The most common problem arises when a man doesn't take enough time for adequate foreplay and clitoral stimulation to arouse his partner fully.

Also, inform your husband frankly that if he comes before you, it's not fair to leave you aroused and unsatisfied. Suggest that he continue to stimulate you by caresses, masturbation, or orally.

After you initiate open, honest communication, both of you should learn to use the Erotic Focus method. As you personally go into E.F. while having sex, and are in this pleasant, floating state, concentrate on your favorite sexual fantasy or the sexual dreams which bring on your orgasms during sleep. Now, while having sex, using the dream material that excited you so much during sleep, odds are that you'll be aroused so intensely that your orgasmic responses will be accelerated—also increasing the intensity of your climaxing. (See "Sexual Fantasies," Chapter 7.)

Here is another way to deal with this problem effectively. As you are aroused from a sexual dream, half-awake and half-asleep in the bed's warmth, awaken your husband gently—tell him you're very "horny," want him very much *"right now."* Few men can refuse such a come-on!

Overwork obstructs sex (man): "I feel *physically and mentally exhausted* after a hard day's work. At night I don't welcome intercourse—that becomes a problem between my wife and me. I want to get ahead in business and need to be refreshed in the morning. What can I do about this dilemma?"

In our world filled with stress and frustration, it happens quite often that people turn off sexually after a long and hard day's work. Here is an easy suggestion to consider: Switch to having sex in the morning. When you wake up, you feel rested, relaxed and refreshed. What better way to start the day than with such an enjoyable activity as sex? Many people find it easier to struggle through the busy hours when they begin with an emotional-physical lift.

Periodic lack of interest (woman): "I think I'm probably about average in my enjoyment of sex, but there are times every few weeks when I just don't feel sexy, and so I turn my husband away. Is it normal that I just don't want to be touched now and then? Should I force myself to have sex anyhow?"

Nobody is sexy all the time. Women seem to experience more variations than men, in general. This may be due to changes in hormonal levels that take place throughout the month, such as "premenstrual syndrome," as well as external circumstances such as tension, over-load, or problems with kids.

Is it fair to your partner to turn him away? Yes and no. Yes, it's okay to say occasionally, "No, not tonight, dear—I'm sorry, I'm just not up to it." But no, you shouldn't deny yourselves the sexual pleasure if the lack of desire can be restored just by overcoming the feelings of stress, fatigue, worry. I suggest that you apply and enjoy the E.F. float in these situations. Its mind-clearing, body-relaxing effects can help you eliminate stressful stumbling blocks, shifting you into a more sexy mood. You'll be delighted with how quickly your energy and desire return.

An example is one of my patients, a hard-working young executive, Laura, who told me she had disap-pointed her husband, Bert, many times sexually. Driv-ing home after a hard day's work, she'd think to herself, "I can't wait until Bert and I have sex to-night."

She went on, "But then I'd say and think—yes, I want to make love *but* I'm so tired . . . *but* I have to get up early tomorrow . . . *but* I have to be alert for the big conference. By the time I arrived home, I felt shot—no desire for sex."

I told Laura, "Each 'but' is like erecting a huge brick wall in front of you, blocking your sexual interest." I taught her the Erotic Focus technique, and suggested that while in the float, she should imagine a huge bull-dozer rolling in and demolishing that built-up brick wall. She'd be freed from being stuck behind that wall of "buts," and then she should concentrate on giving sex full freedom. She applied this process intelligently and soon reported a tremendous sexual resurgence.

Mismatched sexual desire (woman): "I have a fairly satisfying live-in relationship, but there's one big sexual problem and I don't know how to handle it best. My boyfriend is rather shy and lacks sexual aggressiveness. Time after time I want to say, 'Let's make love—I'm hot, I want you inside me,' but I can't speak the words aloud, and I feel deprived and frustrated. How can I open up, and get him to be more assertive?"

It's an outmoded assumption that sexually the *man* must always be the aggressive one. Some men are definitely more passive and shy. They wait for the woman to make the approach. The solution is primarily a simple matter of adjustment—once the woman helps the man to feel comfortable in the relationship, he generally becomes more aggressive.

Keep in mind also that different people have different levels of sexual desire and drive. Perhaps your sex drive is naturally stronger than his, but, whatever the case, it should not be allowed to interfere with your own sexual expression. *Communicate* your dissatisfaction, to help the two of you reach a better match or mix of desire.

This can be a big, practical help: Both of you should go into the E.F. float, and then—relaxed and receptive—start your sex play. Lead him into "playing" the part of a passionate lover. Coach him to exclaim the words of passion that come easily to you but are unaccustomed for him. Often, in play, words of love and passion can be expressed more easily until they pour out naturally from a formerly shy person—and away you go!

"Very little sex" (man): "I'm just past forty, have never married, have had a series of relationships with women, no desire for sex with men. My affairs have never been deep or lasting, and lately I'm content skipping sex for periods, not getting tied down to anybody. Should I just go along enjoying life in a relaxed way as I do, or make the effort to have a more active sex life?"

Basically, you have the right to live your life in *your* most satisfying way. If being on your own is fulfilling, by all means continue. Regarding your sex life, it seems you've always had a relatively low sex drive. Now that you're past forty, it's unlikely that you'll transform into a "stud" who wants sex all the time.

However, you need not spend your life alone. If you search, you will probably find a woman with similar feelings about sex who would happily share her life with you. Humans can enjoy closeness and intimacy even without an intense physical relationship.

Here's a case in point, involving a couple, Mary and Sal, whom I treated a couple of years ago. He'd had a few sexual encounters, but never enjoyed them fully. At forty-nine, he met Mary, thirty-eight, at church. She had dated a bit, but had never had sexual intercourse. She'd masturbate occasionally, only about ten times in the past ten years. After they married, sex became an issue. Neither of them had a strong drive—they just felt pressured to have more sex.

Sal mumbled, "I can't always keep my erections every time. She's a virgin, and I couldn't stay hard enough to break her hymen."

"I went to my gynecologist," Mary threw in, "and he removed my hymen surgically for easier entry by

Sal. We had sex a few times but neither of us enjoyed it much so we stopped for several months. But now we feel we ought to have a child. Since I'm almost past the age, we've tried to have sex, but . . .''

"We love each other," Sal took over, "but we're no good at intercourse. Our gynecologist suggested your help."

They worked at the prescribed sexual treatment steps, but did everything like a school assignment, without real pleasure. Instead, trying to force having sex added pressure that led to bickering. The few times they did complete intercourse didn't result in pregnancy. I suggested fertility tests, which revealed Sal's sperm count was below the normal amount necessary for insemination.

I recommended that they were to use the Erotic Focus method up to ten times daily, individually and/or together. This would relieve the pressure and help them clarify their thoughts, *focusing on what each really wanted out of life*.

When they returned to my office, I was pleased to see new self-assurance on their faces, and intimacy in their bearing. Mary explained, "Thank you, we're now at peace. We realize that it was really our families who were pushing us hard to have a child. Now we're resolved that at our age *we* don't need or want a baby. As for sex—it's not that important to either of us—we love most just to kiss and cuddle."

Sal added, "When that leads to intercourse, fine—but we can take it or leave it."

They smiled at each other contentedly. I agreed that it was their right to enjoy life their way. I still receive cards from them at holidays which reflect a very happy union.

Must loving be a hassle? (man): "I've had a fairly satisfactory live-in relationship with an attractive woman for several years. The last few months, I've lost my desire to make love. I'd rather take a relaxing bath or an energetic walk, to avoid the hassle of getting it up whether I'm in the mood or not, saying I love her, acting excited, all that guff. My partner wants it whenever *she* feels like it, and resents my attitude. Is there a solution for us?"

Sex is a normal human drive, the same as the urge to eat, drink or sleep. If suddenly, your sex drive which was normal before, drops significantly and you see loving as a chore rather than a pleasure, you should *reexamine your feelings* for your girlfriend, or consider that your lack of sexual desire may be an indication of *something else occurring*. Maybe it's an early symptom of depression, or extreme stress or worries on the job.

Examine your feelings thoroughly. Use the focused concentration of E.F. to help think it through, then as an aid to get back to your original state of sexual interest. Also have your partner join you in using sexual fantasies, sex games, different positions to add variety to your sex life. Goodbye "hassle!" By just "performing and making believe," you make the situation worse. *Talk it out!* If you two can't communicate, is the relationship worth continuing?

Sex and marriage (couple): "We've been living together for over two years, and enjoying very good sex. There's no question about our mutual love. We think we're ready for marriage, except for one doubt: some friends say that pleasure in sex diminishes with married life. What are the facts about marriage and sexual pleasure?''

Since you've been living together for two years, doesn't that mean that in a way you're ''married'' already? By getting officially married, all you do is make it a legally more binding contract. That really shouldn't influence your sexual enjoyment with each other.

If your friends say that sex deteriorates in marriage, maybe they talk out of their own perspective. Marriages *and* relationships have problems, and it's up to the individual couple to solve them. These research findings may be helpful to you:

- Married people, in general, have a more regular and satisfying sex life than singles
- Sex is more rewarding for most in an emotionally meaningful, trusting relationship—married or not
- Sex, although a natural function of the body, gets better if a couple works at it and finds variety and mutual pleasuring, usually developing over a period of time

Finally, it will be up to *you*—not your ''friends''—to make marriage a thorough success if you undertake it. Consider all angles (doing so in the relaxing, clarifying state of Erotic Focus can help), then make your *personal* decision.

Is promiscuity the answer? (woman): ''I've lived with a man for over a year now, and neither of us is thrilled with our sex life together. We make love, have our piddly orgasms, then go to sleep dissatisfied. Maybe if we cheat, each learning some new tricks, we can teach each other and make sex together great. Is that the way to go?''

"Cheating," no. There are two basic directions to go:

1. Improve your relationship with one another.

2. Get out of the situation as soon as possible—split.

Getting sexually involved promiscuously with other people rarely, if ever, solves problems like yours. Here's what I suggest:

a) Learn the Erotic Focus method. Use the "video screen technique" to project things *you feel are missing in the relationship.* Then, project those aspects which *you* consider are positive strong points that hold you together. That two-step approach will clarify for you the direction to take. Tell your partner what you've come up with—discuss all facets thoroughly.

For example, perhaps one factor bothering you is that you're *bored* with the monotony, always in the missionary position (man on top). Then have fun creating and trying alternatives . . . add sexual fantasies, games (Chapters 7 and 8).

b) Also use E.F. *while having sex* to be in full contact with all feelings, enhancing your senses, enjoying each action thoroughly.

If all this doesn't help, either try for an understanding of your problem through professional help, or question whether you really want this relationship. If not, act to dissolve it.

Apprehensive about women's advances (man): "I've always managed okay at intercourse, lots of pleasure for both. But my new girlfriend makes me doubt my masculinity. As we start making love, she is all over me like a human octopus. She comes on so strong that instead of enjoying her fervor, my penis goes limp. How can I cope?''

Consider various reasons why she is overaggressive sexually. Perhaps she's overanxious to please you. She may wish to make you feel *wanted*. Furthermore, the new ''sexual freedom'' and so-called sexual revolution make some women think they have to be the aggressive ones. If this turns you off, *tell her*.

In a good relationship, sexual aggression or initiative should be mutual. At times, the woman should be the aggressive one; at other times, the man. The couple should find mutually satisfying agreement on this. To create the compromise, you must communicate and work at the solution. If you find it difficult to speak up, rehearse your approach first in the E.F. float. This will make it clearer and easier to arrive at the best way for both.

Body massage turn-on (man): ''My ex-wife (we're divorced) used to turn me on with an all-over body massage. My new live-in girlfriend refuses to massage me, insists I must learn how to erect 'normally.' I can't make it that way. I don't want to lose her. What can I do?''

It's understandable why your new partner rejects your ''required'' body massage. If you can get an erection only this way, you make her feel like a mere apparatus to provide an erection, rather than your responding to her as a loving individual. Sexual habits are *learned,* and you've conditioned yourself to get aroused only by massage.

Here's my advice: Practice the E.F. method. While relaxed and focused, think back and recall getting an erection other ways since your teens—before this massage pattern developed. You did okay without massage, didn't you? And you can again!

Next, visualize yourself (in your E.F. state) getting erections with your new partner in ways that *she* prefers. Look at every inch of her nude body and let the thrills (and your penis) build. Gradually you'll train yourself to many new ways of erecting, erasing the old habitual reflex. More fun!

Also, get closer to her by talking over how to change the massage habit. Work on it *together.* Go into Erotic Focus with her . . . let your body float freely, pleasurably . . . and you'll find your penis doing what comes naturally with the total, exciting involvement of your partner.

Sex with lights on (woman): "Guess I'm still a strict convent girl at heart, so our new marriage is becoming a sexual horror. Before the wedding, we had great intercourse—in a parked car, on the dark porch, secretive places—sneaky but fun. Now he says he likes it best in bed under a spotlight, facing a big mirror. I get embarrassed, it's a disaster. How can I give in or change him?"

Your embarrassment may actually be part of the enjoyment your husband gets from sex spotlighted in a mirror. Apparently he gets a special kick out of watching your twisting body and flushed face fully illuminated. Many people are like your husband and enjoy sex with lights on. That in itself shouldn't be a problem. So let's look further.

Think, are you shy about your body? That may be due to lack of experience, along with your inbred moral values. You should start right now, don't wait, to open up and talk about all this together. Tell him exactly how you feel, and vice versa. Love finds mutually satisfying compromises . . . like turning the lights down some, or using candlelight instead of spotlights . . . or alternating with sex in the dark.

The bottom line is to make love in ways you *both* go for—always open to explore new thrills, deeper gratification. Prepare by visualizing sexual variety in repeated Erotic Focus adventures when you're exceptionally aware. Zoom into E.F. right before sex, and let go. Joyous sex can light up your lives!

Sexual Attitudes

"Normal" frequency (couple): **"We've been having intercourse about once a week and enjoying it. We've just read that the 'normal' average for people in their thirties is three times a week. We're concerned—does that mean that we're undersexed?"**

Studies of marital satisfaction show, as I can't overemphasize, that it's not the *amount* of sex that matters, but the *quality* and feelings of closeness and intimacy that are part of better sex. If you've developed a pattern of sex once a week, and that one occasion is fully satisfying for both of you, that's great. "Normal" frequency is what is right and normal to *you two*. Don't be concerned about statistics on frequency of couples' sexual intercourse. Figures vary considerably, and the dependability of answers is debatable because of the possibility of exaggeration by those questioned.

Here's a suggestion that may increase your pleasure: A satisfying sexual relationship is a good base from which to experiment with your own sexuality. Very often, people get caught in a pattern and don't even question the possibility of boosting their enjoyment. How about the two of you using the Erotic Focus method to add to your fun? You can explore sexual fantasies and experiment with some of the sex games described. The bonus is that if you're creative with "good" sex, it becomes *better sex!*

Fear of "satyriasis," being oversexed (male): "I'm a successful executive, but my thoughts concentrate increasingly on sex. My appetite appears insatiable, intercourse with up to four different women a day. Do I have *satyriasis?* What should I do about it?"

Satyriasis is the male counterpart to female nymphomania—excessive sexual excitement and behavior. There's no solid consensus on what is excessive. Sexual desire and activity vary with each man, and according to age. A seventeen-year-old male who wants sex "all the time" isn't necessarily oversexed. In contrast, if a grown man is so obsessed with sex that he neglects his work and responsibilities, that probably is considered "excessive."

If *your* sexual appetite doesn't interfere with your handling of responsibilities, you probably needn't be concerned. However, it could indicate that *you're not fully satisfied with your love relationships,* and perhaps should find a steady partner.

Starting now, use the E.F. inner screen technique to act out some sexual encounters just in your mind, rather than chasing women too much. Examining yourself "in action" could also provide insights to why you find yourself thinking so much about sex. Finally, if your sex drive becomes a pressing problem, interfering with your life, do consider professional help.

Is sado-masochism normal? (woman): "My boyfriend wants us to try sadomasochism, tying me down, beating me lightly with a whip, having me pretend to scream in terror, all that. He says that 'it's the thing to do these days, everybody's doing it, and orgasms become supersensational.' It goes against my grain. Shall I give in, or give up my man's company which I enjoy as a whole?"

Some "normal" people enjoy "harmless" sadomasochistic sexual fantasies and/or activities. If your boyfriend requests some new ways of making love, *you should consent only if you feel comfortable with them,* especially with sadomasochistic pursuits. Some S-M forms can be very arousing as part of the lovemaking repertoire. You apparently have a good relationship, and don't want to give him up just because of this request.

Here are two possibilities to consider:

1. Tell your boyfriend to *fantasize* that you beat or bite or scratch him while making love, without the actual physical actions.

2. Analyze your concerns about S-M activities. Go into the E.F. float, and on your inner screen, project as actuality the activities he suggests. Imagine that you

lightly spank or whip or restrain him . . . and vice versa. Consider, are any of these forms acceptable and pleasurable for you?

If you decide "yes," then you might try these pursuits occasionally in your lovemaking routine, rather than simply reject something due to fear or lack of true information. Think about it, then decide about the value of the relationship, along with your own sensibilities. Also, check S-M in Chapter 8.

Infidelity in a relationship (man): **"My partner and I aren't married but we have had a two-year relationship, living together. A month ago she told me that she went to bed with another man while away on a business trip. I find myself increasingly jealous and now shy away from sex with her—yet we still love each other. Can you help?"**

A good start for you is to realize that it's not easy to come to terms with a partner's "infidelity," whether in a marriage or a live-in relationship. Try to think it through clearly (using the Erotic Focus technique can help clarify your insights). Consider this: Your partner chose to be honest.

Doesn't that show you that *the affair meant less to her* than your relationship? She came back to *you*. How about getting it out in the open? Admit that it hurt you deeply. Perhaps together you can set some rules that you both can accept and live with.

Simply feeling resentful and avoiding sex is rather childish, isn't it? That's like a pouting little boy holding on to his "toy," not letting her "play with it." If you still love each other, you'll overcome the hurt as you talk it out and forgive.

Oral sex (man): "My wife wants me to have oral sex to bring her to climax. That seems unclean to me. I can't do it. She's frustrated, says I'm a prig. What do you suggest?"

Try to examine your resistance against oral sex. You say it's "unclean"—is that true if your wife showers and bathes regularly? The genitals are generally more protected from outside contamination than the hands and mouth—yet, do you avoid touching and kissing? For some, a woman's genitals, with their particular scent, are "strange," therefore disagreeable and to be avoided.

Have you considered looking at oral sex as expansion and innovation in your sex life? The Playboy Foundation has found that 80 percent of single males and females under thirty-five, and 90 percent of married couples, have experienced oral sex. Many people engage in oral sex, and apparently find it enjoyable. Shouldn't you give yourself a chance to explore it?

Consider this step-by-step "desensitization" strategy:

1. In your Erotic Focus float, project a sexual image on your inner screen, imagining how it would feel, look and taste if you were to kiss your wife's genitals. Then, think of how it would feel if she were kissing and sucking your penis. After "rehearsing" this in E.F. several times, discuss with her your feelings, and the possibility of experimenting. If you start slowly with oral sex, you may feel comfortable and willing to enjoy it.

2. Before actually participating, take a bath or a shower together so you *know* you're both physically clean. Agree to speak up if either of you becomes too

uncomfortable, then turn to more familiar forms of lovemaking until next time.

3. To begin, get comfortable, and go into E.F. to be fully relaxed. Proceed to kiss her stomach area, thighs, pubic hair . . . brush your lips lightly over her genitals, and again . . . but more intensely, no rush, no competition.

Now take turns. Both go into E.F. She should gently caress and kiss your abdomen, thighs, penis . . . licking lightly, more urgently, finally sucking until you come, inside her mouth or not (make sure beforehand, since some women don't enjoy ejaculation in the mouth). If you both enjoy oral sex, you may wish to pleasure each other simultaneously. *Mutual agreement is always the key!*

Try group sex? (woman): **"My boyfriend wants us both to join in group sex. When I said I couldn't go for that, he threatened a breakup. I'd hate to lose him since he has many good qualities and we get along great. Should I try it?"**

You should get involved in group sex only if you feel that you definitely want to and can handle it emotionally and if you're willing to take the physical responsibilities of possibly contracting herpes or other sexually transmitted diseases. In group sex you know little about the participants' sex practices and involvements, compared with one partner, and are taking a far greater risk.

Emotionally you gamble too! It can be very destructive to a relationship to see your boyfriend having sex with another woman or man, or with both simultaneously. Yes, some people are greatly aroused by watching others have sex and being stimulated by a man and a woman concurrently.

Obviously, however, you're not comfortable with the whole idea. Ask your boyfriend why having group sex is important to him, when sex is a private, intimate, shared experience for most. There may be a hidden message here. Perhaps all he needs is some creative addition, more variety in your sexual relationship.

Positive step one might be to *enlarge your sexual activities with him*—not with more people. Read Chapters 7 and 8 on "Sexual Fantasies" and "Sex Games" and discuss the possibilities thoroughly with him. There's likely to be a tragic outcome, emotionally and physically, in engaging in sexual adventuring against your will.

Watch sex movies? (man): "My wife keeps renting sexually explicit cassettes to show on our videotape player. She wants us to watch them nude together. She says it turns her on, but it turns me off. Who's right, who's wrong? What should I do?"

It seems clear that your wife is trying to give you a message: *She wants more variety and excitement in your sex life together.* Has sex become routine for her? Does she need additional stimulation to get aroused? Give that serious thought, instead of being angry, resentful, turned off. Ask yourself how to improve and add spice to your intercourse.

If sex movies don't turn you on, be creative and adventurous—suggest to her what *you* want to do. Use the Erotic Focus method to get in touch with your innermost wishes and desires. I'm convinced from similar experiences with patients that you'll find something to suggest to her to make your mutual sex life more stimulating and satisfying for both, without resorting to movies that alienate you.

Marry a bisexual/homosexual—or a transvestite? (woman): "My boyfriend and I have had pretty good occasional sex. Mostly we enjoy each other's company and living together. Now he has admitted that he's bisexual, and wants me to marry him to help him give up men. Can I realistically expect him to do that? And will he be satisfied with sex just with me?"

Some people get married despite the fact that one partner is bisexual, that is, attracted to both sexes. Keep this in mind: Getting married in itself does not change a person's sexual preference. Your boyfriend seems to have that unrealistic expectation. I strongly recommend that he go for expert professional help before you make that commitment. *He should work out his sexual problem before getting married.* Experience proves that you can't tackle this by yourself effectively.

Sex with two partners? (man): "My live-in partner for years has been wonderful in every way, great sex. But now I'm concerned. She suggested bringing a 'sexy lady' home with her—and having a threesome. For me, it would turn love into an animalistic grappling match. We love each other—I'm sure this is just a passing fancy. How can I convince her that twosome sex is perfect for us?"

Women have visited me about a similar problem—a threesome with two men. The answer is about the same. There can be various reasons why one partner suggests a threesome. Sometimes it's just an attempt to add change and spice to the relationship. Or there can be an underlying homosexual (lesbian) attraction. Whatever it is, it should be done *only if all three partners involved feel fully comfortable* with such a setup.

If one or two of those involved don't feel right, it definitely should not be done. This situation can be very destructive if forced on someone. If you don't want it, assert your right to say no conclusively. In this instance, suggest that your girlfriend use sexual fantasy herself while in E.F., as a threesome substitute. While having sex with you, she could imagine that "sexy lady" fondling her (but keeping it to herself).

Alarmed about anal intercourse (woman): **"After a year of loving, live-in companionship and terrific sex, my partner wants to try entering my anus for intercourse. I find this repulsive, and I am afraid of the pain too. How can I persuade him to just enjoy normal sex?"**

Many couples engage occasionally in anal intercourse, and most women find it exciting. If you never had anal intercourse, and your rectal sphincter (the muscle that keeps your anus closed) is very tight, it could feel uncomfortable. If your partner uses a lubricant, and is gentle, it needn't be painful. But if you tense up, it will hurt.

You alone can decide about acceptance or rejection of anal intercourse. If you do try it, go into E.F. right before—to be fully relaxed so he can enter you slowly (the sphincter muscle relaxes automatically after the penis has been inserted). If you proceed, discuss it thoroughly first. Have him go gently, stopping once his penis is a little inside you, then, as your sphincter eases up, his penis will slide in gradually. Anal intercourse should never be undertaken without your full consent and cooperation.

Wear blatantly sexy outfits? (woman): **"My husband read a book that says I should be waiting for him at home in a see-through negligee or other obscene outfits he bought. He says it turns him on, and that I owe him. I find it demeaning. How can I make it right for both of us?"**

Sexy clothes on a woman turn on many men. But you should wear them only if you feel comfortable doing so. If your husband has made these demands only lately, perhaps he's trying to give you a message. Maybe he's not sexually satisfied, and wants some variety in your lovemaking. Why not try this:

Tell your man that you don't like the sexy clothes bit, but that you too would welcome some added spice in your sexual life. Have fun discussing together ways to discover new dimensions sexually, with new twists that are *mutually* acceptable and stirring.

Also apply the E.F. method to become more aware of your sexual desires and possibilities. Project pictures on your inner screen, perhaps actually wearing the sexy nothings. In your relaxed state, not angry or antagonistic, you might get a laugh and new thrills wearing them. Think about it, pro and con.

If you're still negative, speak up. I'm sure he never intended to put you down. Offer alternate stimulating suggestions. Together read about innovative "sex games" (Chapter 8) and play out what attracts and excites you both. Have a ball!

Sex for joy? (woman): "I was brought up very strictly to think that sex is just for having babies—period. I'm recently married, and my husband says that sex is also for expressing love, for sheer joy and having fun. I can't seem to let go totally so we both get the fullest pleasure. How can I break free?"

I hope you'll read this book thoroughly from cover to cover. Then it will be crystal clear to you that sex has *two* major functions: Procreation of the human race . . . and j-o-y. Your husband shares the opinion of most people that sex is a *primary* way of communicating love and closeness. If you're not joyous in coupling, you'll miss a most important aspect of marriage: *union.*

Try to separate yourself from past constrictions. Being grown up means at some level recognizing that your values can be different from those of your parents, and still be *your* best choice. There's no absolute "right" or "wrong" here. Seek intelligently what is *right for you,* not accepting others' views blindly, regardless of respect for them as individuals.

Go into the E.F. float, and use the revealing screen technique several times a day. Study and analyze the how and why of ingrained feelings from the past. Critically examine if they really apply to *you here and now,* assessing *their validity today for you.* Then, make your personal decision.

Sexual Response

Multiple orgasms (woman): "**Most of the time I climax once. My live-in lover now has read about 'multiple orgasms,' and he's after me to come repeatedly each time. I'm honest, I can't fake a series like that. Maybe I'm not trying hard enough. Am I wrong—or is he—and what can I do about it?**"

Your lover should not pressure you and I suggest that you discuss the following with him. The first point to understand is that *quantity is not necessarily quality.* If you have just one fully satisfying orgasm during each sexual encounter, that's probably just right for you. If your partner keeps pushing you to have more orgasms, ask him exactly what that means to him, why it's so important. Ask why he thinks more is better. Why is he "keeping score?"

Explain that some women (not a large percentage) have multiple orgasms, that is, several orgasms following each other with scarcely a pause between. The enjoyment women get from this type of orgasm *is not necessarily greater*—actually, some women describe this machine-gun activity as almost painful. A *single* orgasm can be very intense and satisfying.

Furthermore, not having multiple orgasms is no reflection on either partner. It has nothing to do with "not trying hard enough" (the harder you try, the less likely that it will happen). Orgasm is basically a muscle reflex. Triggered in a specific way, and once started, it takes its course. If you have multiple orgasms, it means that the trigger repeats itself a few times, like a broken record—each time the needle hits that one point, the record "hiccups" again and again.

You should feel good about the way you are, but if you still want to see if you can teach your body to have multiple orgasms, try the following:

1. First, before intercourse, go into your E.F. float, to feel fully relaxed, physically and mentally in "neutral gear." Then tell your partner that he should continue to stimulate you manually or orally around your clitoris *right after you come*. Since you just had an orgasm and are very excited, such manipulation may bring you quickly to a second or third climax.

2. Fantasize on your own by going into E.F. several times during the day or evening, and "imagine" in your E.F. state what it would feel like having a multiple orgasm, your body responding time after time. Visualize this on your inner TV screen watching yourself come repeatedly in a "behavior rehearsal." Feeling what it would be like should make it easier to achieve in real life.

3. "Faking" multiple orgasms is inadvisable. If people can't be truthful with each other during this most intimate activity, when can you be honest? Rather than faking it, tell your partner frankly that you have not experienced multiple orgasms so far—but that perhaps the two of you can "role play" it together, bringing you both even closer.

After your E.F. "behavior rehearsals," as you become more familiar with the experience, try it in cooperation with your partner. This is totally different from "faking." This trying can be exciting and stimulating extra fun. Eventually it may lead to multiple orgasms that you both enjoy. In any case, your *mutual* orgasms should be better than ever due to experimenting *together*.

Mutual, simultaneous orgasms (man): "My live-in girlfriend and I enjoy what we consider very good sex. We both have satisfying orgasms, but we climax simultaneously only once in a while. It's especially great when that happens but we've never cared who came first up to now. Others insist that simultaneous orgasms are the only way to go. How can we have mutual orgasms every time?"

The goal you set of having mutual simultaneous orgasms all the time is unrealistic. There will always be occasions when one or the other partner cannot, or does not want to, hold back—and just comes. That's fine—both can enjoy it.

Also many couples get special pleasure from "watching" the other partner climax, as one is holding back. This gives both individuals a special sense of sharing and giving.

In your case, if it is your aim to increase your frequency of mutual simultaneous orgasms, it should be relatively easy to accomplish this way:

1. Practice the E.F. technique until you both have it down pat and enjoy the relaxing, energizing float thoroughly.

2. Go into E.F. before you start having sex. Since being in E.F. increases your focused concentration on your physical sensations and body movements you'll both find it easier to each maintain *control* and to hold off orgasm until you are *both* ready to peak. When both

are about to get there, *say so loud and clear* . . . and then
. . . *wham,* together!

Follow that course again and again—and you should
dramatically increase the number of times you climax
together. Since you both want that, it should boost your
total sensual pleasure.

Rushing an orgasm (woman): **"When having sex,
I'm always fearful that my partner is trying to hold
back in order to make me come first—and that if I
take too long he'll become angry with me. So I try to
pressure myself into orgasm, but the more I try, the
longer I take. How can I manage to climax sooner?"**

Sex is not a "race" or a "performance." That's why
usually you cannot climax quickly if you try hard to do
so. That makes you, in effect, an observer rather than a
participant. But don't worry about it; you can generally overcome your problem easily in this way:

Basically, realize that women normally take longer to
be aroused. Now, ask yourself: "Does my partner allow enough time for foreplay and touching, so that by
the time he penetrates with his penis, I'm fully
aroused?" Probably you'll find that he doesn't, that he
just speeds ahead. Discuss this with him, get his viewpoint.

If he does arouse you fully, but you still take longer
than he does to climax, try the following: Go into E.F.
so your body becomes fully relaxed, and your mind
clears away your performance anxiety. Odds are that
when your body is in the focused awareness state of
E.F., orgasm will occur more readily and intensely.

If climaxing still takes you longer than him, talk over
the possibility of his holding back his orgasm when he is

ready to come. If he cannot, he should climax first—*and then stimulate you* either orally, through masturbation with extra clitoral stimulation and/or with a vibrator until you too climax. Then you're both more than satisfied.

Holding back orgasm (man): "I've heard so much about women being unsatisfied sexually because of a man's premature ejaculation, that I try to hold back until my partner comes. My problem is that when I hold back, I often lose my erection, then the whole situation goes bad. How can I restrain myself from coming too soon, and still keep my erection until my partner is satisfied?"

Premature ejaculation becomes a problem if you don't fully arouse your partner before entering her or if you don't get her to climax at all because, after you come, you stop and let her hang there unfulfilled. Instead, bring her to climax as I've recommended in the preceding answer.

Now, about your loss of erection—that seems to be precipitated by *performance anxiety.* You observe yourself, instead of just floating along with the building excitation. Try this: Go into E.F. while having sex, then concentrate on the sensations your penis is giving you. Enjoy the throbbing, pleasurable thrusting inside your partner . . .

If you come before her, that's okay—just bring her to orgasm in the other ways I've advised. If there's another "round," you'll find your erection lasting longer; the first orgasm naturally comes quickest.

Another suggestion: You'd probably benefit from

doing the sexual exercises for men (Chapter 9) to gain additional control as a result of your muscles being strengthened around your penis and the floor of your pelvis.

Where to touch? (man): "I'm bewildered by all the stuff I read about massaging a woman's clitoris, her cervix, uterus, her vagina, her 'G-spot,' if that exists, and who knows what else. When I ask my girlfriend where and how to caress, she says, 'Just do it your way.' Where shall I touch, and how, to help bring her to her greatest orgasms? I want to be the most terrific lover but I don't know how."

Here are a few basic helps: Most women like to be touched, *especially when already sexually aroused,* around the *clitoris*—the erectile organ at the upper end of the vulva, the external female genitalia, at the entrance of the *vagina,* around the *nipples.* These are the primary *genital arousal zones.* (See diagram in Chapter 9.)

Note these guidelines also: The *vagina deep inside* is not very sensitive to touch. The *cervix,* all the way in at the end of the vagina, is completely insensitive to touch, and is usually not reached by the exploring finger. The *uterus is inside the pelvic cavity* and not reachable from the vagina. "G-spot" is a controversial term, and it remains unknown whether this, in fact, is an arousal zone.

There are additional body areas sexually arousable to touch. These are usually referred to as the "erogenous zones," located at various spots in the body—particularly at the bottom of the neck, at the back . . .

the ears ("Blow in my ear and I'll follow you anywhere") . . . the underarms . . . the insides of the thighs . . . other places. Individual responses vary, so touch all over together, and the varied reactions will tell you which are the most pleasurable zones. Fun for both, and better sex indeed.

Increase potency by abstinence? (man): "Lately it has taken me longer to have an erection, and I wonder whether having sex about twice a week is too much to expect (I'm forty-five). If I cut down to sex once a week or so, have I a better chance to be more potent and get a strong erection more readily?"

Lest you become overly concerned about your potency, consider the general facts. Physical changes occur in males and females in respect to sexual responsiveness and the aging process. Over sixty, most men take longer to achieve full erection. There is also a decrease in the force of the ejaculation, and a lengthening of the refractory (repeat) period. Occasionally there may be ejaculation before full erection has occurred. With the refractory phase prolonged, if an erection is lost during the excitement phase, or after orgasm, it may take up to several hours to get another erection. However, because of the increased time of getting a full erection, the man's *excitement phase* is longer, with more extended sexual arousal and excitation.

At your age, forty-five, most men have their customary physical responses. I suspect that you are very *anxious* about changes that are not there yet but that you anticipate. Or perhaps you've had occasional difficulty in achieving full erection, and so you tend to worry about it.

Specifically, *abstinence does not increase potency*. If anything, the old saying holds true: "If you don't use it, you lose it." If your regular sexual activity has been twice a week, and you desire that, *by all means keep it that way*.

To assuage your concerns, using E.F. can be especially helpful. I recommend that you go into E.F. for general relaxation and uplift—and also do it *right before* having sexual intercourse. This will help you to reduce your performance and/or abstinence anxiety, and will allow your natural sexuality to have full play.

Then, during sexual intercourse, concentrate on the very pleasurable feelings aroused in your penis. *Enjoy* the fact that it may take a little longer to get a full erection, because that means your excitement phase is *prolonged*. Thus, you can experience *more* pleasure, especially now that your enjoyment won't be diminished by negative worrisome anxiety.

In addition, you can improve the tone of your pelvic muscles (see Chapter 9). This has a positive influence on the strength of your erection and your thrusting ability.

As further reassurance, reputable studies about the frequency of sexual intercourse in later years show most males and females over age forty-five at "once a week", about half that number reporting "two to three times a week", and quite a few disclosing "more than three times a week." Do I see a smile of relief and pleasurable anticipation on your face?

Using a vibrator (woman): "Since my divorce, my sexual experience has been limited to masturbation, which doesn't satisfy me. A woman friend urges me to buy a vibrator. She says she gets terrific orgasms that way, but it seems mechanical and contrived to me. Also, I'm afraid it might spoil my future relations with men. Is that valid, or is it okay for me to experiment?"

Some women are hesitant to use a vibrator, fearing they'll get "hooked" on it, and not enjoy sexual intercourse anymore. Using a vibrator may add a new, pleasant experience sexually, since you haven't a partner currently. There's no evidence that women who use vibrators will prefer it to sexual satisfaction with a partner.

Once you have a new man in your life, you may store it away, or you and your partner may want to add it to your sexual repertoire. Many couples enjoy using a vibrator as an alternative and/or part of sexual stimulation. There's a difference between orgasms alone with a vibrator and through sexual intercourse.

Usually a woman using a vibrator will climax quite speedily, probably due to the mechanical, regular, quick motion boosting muscle reflex contraction. Most important, a vibrator is no substitute for the intimacy of the human sexual encounter. If you enjoy that, don't worry about getting bonded to the vibrator. Consider it a temporary form of relief, probably preferable to abstinence and frustration in having no sexual outlet.

If you use a vibrator, try going into the E.F. float: Fantasize about being with a loving partner, past or future. You'll get greater pleasure, and minimize the mechanical aspects of vibrator orgasm.

Does menstruation bar intercourse? (woman): "My live-in partner wants intercourse even when I'm menstruating. That seems 'dirty' to me, goes against my grain. I'm afraid of risking some internal injury, too. And isn't one more likely to become pregnant while menstruating? Yet when he kisses and strokes me when I'm menstruating, I get hot and want him in me. What should I do?"

Sex during menstrual flow is in no way medically harmful, despite many myths. In some cultures, a woman is considered "unclean," and must wait ten days until after the last drop of blood. Then she must have a ritual cleansing bath before resuming intercourse.

Some women feel *increased* sexual desire during menstruation. Unless her lover finds the blood frightening or unesthetic, there's no reason not to enjoy intercourse. It's entirely a matter of esthetic and personal preference whether to refrain or not.

Apparently you feel aroused physically but reject the idea because of preconceived and medically unfounded reasons. Try this: Go into E.F. to relax, up to ten times daily. Also, when you are menstruating, and you and your partner feel like having intercourse, go into E.F. float beforehand—when your flow is not heaviest. Let any tension ease, and as your lover enters you, let go!

About becoming pregnant: ovulation usually takes place about ten to fourteen days after the previous menstrual period, so you're relatively safe during menstruation (but not surely). Spontaneous ovulation can occur almost any time—rare, but possible, with reports of some women becoming pregnant. On the pill, danger is minimal (but still possible), as ovulation is suppressed.

If you usually use a diaphragm, or an IUD, you may also suggest that your partner wear a condom during sexual intercourse. A double advantage is that you get extra protection against becoming pregnant and your partner won't get blood on his penis.

Afraid of penis shrinking yearly (man): "I'm not yet fifty, virile and potent, but I understand that the penis shrinks with age. I might joke that I'm wearing it out, but am I in danger of losing my sexual ability? My anxiety is no joke."

You're virile and potent, so no need to be anxious. With an active sex life, and a willing partner, your sexual abilities can continue indefinitely. There are some changes with advancing age, such as prolonged time between erections, less ejaculate, and perhaps a slight decrease in drive. Atrophy or shrinking may occur slightly, due to loss of strength and tone in tissues. Similarly, arm, leg and buttock muscles may get a bit sluggish and flabby. But such changes are minute, should *not* interfere with your potency and enjoyment of sex.

What can interfere is high anxiety. Learn the Erotic Focus method. Go into E.F. several times daily for mental relaxation and refreshment. Also take a quickie E.F. break just before any stressful times. Above all, don't shrink away from sex!

Marijuana killing erection (male): "I need help urgently! I enjoy smoking grass, and it makes me horny. But when I go to insert my penis, I lose my erection. As a substitute, my girl refuses to have oral sex. Must I give up smoking dope?''

The active chemical ingredient in marijuana is *tetrahydrocannabinol*, a mild hallucinogenic drug. Effects on the sexual response vary with the individual. If smoking grass makes you horny but kills your erection, shouldn't you try sex without smoking, in a way that's arousing and maintains your erection? Go into E.F. and use sexual imagery, a great turn-on for most. Then insert your erect penis, and away you both go!

Your girlfriend probably refuses oral sex because she feels you prefer marijuana to her, making her feel like an object, an available apparatus. Ask yourself, ''Is my 'trip' really necessary?'' She may enjoy oral sex for arousal and even orgasm in exciting lovemaking, but without pot. Try it and see.

Foods for love? (man): ''A friend who thinks she knows everything about nutrition insists that I eat certain things—ginseng and special vitamins and minerals and other so-called health items. She says they'll boost my sexual appetite and my performance and endurance in bed. What are the facts?''

The best food for love is being in love! As of now, there is no clear evidence that there is any specific food or potion that makes people more sexually interested or potent. If anything, eating a large amount of food before sex might interfere with sexual enjoyment since a person who has overeaten may feel weighed down, sleepy, and not at all eager to engage in sex.

Of course a person should be well nourished in general and take care of his body in every respect. If you are in good physical condition, you're likely to enjoy the physical aspects of sex more fully than if you're in poor shape and poop out quickly. But don't count on any one food, such as oysters, to make you more virile. As Lord Byron wrote, even "an oyster may be crossed in love!"

Need an aphrodisiac? (man): "Maybe I'm undersexed, but I really don't think so. I have a fairly active sex life. Yet when I'm with an attractive woman and she's obviously available for sex, I have little desire at times and don't take advantage of the opportunity. Should I seek some kind of aphrodisiac, or is there any other way I can increase my sexual appetite?"

If you have a fairly active sex life but find that at times you lack desire, especially when a woman makes herself readily available, *I suggest you try to figure out exactly what turns you off.* It could be that you want to pursue a woman rather than be pursued, and if a "conquest" is too easy, you lose interest.

The best aphrodisiac for most people is to be in love. And perhaps that's what is missing in your relationships. Just because a woman is "available" doesn't mean you really want her. And just having sex because it's there for the taking can be as inappropriate or meaningless as if you stuff in food just because it's in front of you—in spite of not being at all hungry.

Forget taking an aphrodisiac pill or potion to automatically increase your sexual desire—there's no such easy answer. If my preceding comments don't satisfy you, try sexual fantasizing with the aid of E.F. (detailed in Chapter 7). This can add to your arousal reactions on those occasions when sex is available but lacks an essential bit of excitement that's missing for you now. Above all, give thought to looking within yourself more deeply, as suggested.

Is adult spanking unhealthy? (woman): "Every once in a while, my husband and I have a heavy quarrel which usually winds up with my apologizing for picking on him. We agree mutually then that I should be spanked. He puts me over his lap, and spanks me soundly but never violently, just enough so I feel chastised. It's a turn-on for both of us, followed by unusually exciting intercourse. Is this perverted and unnatural, harmful or dangerous emotionally? Is it okay to continue—or should we stop the spanking completely?"

It's not infrequent that a couple gets turned on sexually after an argument or fight. This usually means that they both want to make up, and sex is one way of communicating that desire. It seems that you have developed this little ritual or ceremony mutually to reconcile after a quarrel.

You say that you both enjoy it, and that you keep it within limits . . . that your husband spanks you in a way that doesn't really hurt. That's play rather than real punishment. If this is your way of clearing the air, and it works so satisfactorily, why not? But, if the actions accelerate so that pain enters the equation, *beware*, take stock before serious physical and emotional hurt is inflicted. (See "Kinky Sex," Chapter 8.)

Lust for young girls (man): "I have a pressing problem that's getting worse. I'm a family man, fine wife, two teenage daughters. I have this urgent desire to fondle little girls of about ten, and to expose myself to them. So far I've controlled myself from having sex with them, but I fear that eventually I'll cross the line. Help!''

Your cry for help is an encouraging sign. It's not so uncommon to have a fleeting fantasy of some form of sexual activity that's not socially accepted. Most people just put it out of mind. With your fantasies becoming more frequent, and feeling a strong urge to *act* upon these impulses, I recommend professional help immediately to avoid tragic consequences!

You need a professional psychotherapist to help you analyze these feelings, understand what they mean, how to counteract them. *Pedophilia* (sexual attraction to children) and *exhibitionism* (getting sexual gratification by exposing the genitals in public) are *sexual deviations of serious consequences that should be treated without delay.* Check Chapter 14, to help find the right therapist for you.

Sexual Fears and Insecurities

Fear of disease (woman): ''Reading the frightening reports in all media about 'epidemics' of herpes, syphilis, gonorrhea, AIDS, and other possibilities of contagion, I've become too scared to have sex with a man. It seems that masturbation is the only safe sex, but it doesn't satisfy me; it's lonely and inadequate for me. How can I overcome my fear and resultant isolation?''

With sexually transmitted diseases on the rise, it

need not mean to you, or to other women and men, that the only safe sexual activity is masturbation. Here are suggestions:

Be very selective in choosing a partner.

Be extra-careful about getting involved with several different partners—that increases the risk of disease.

Before having sexual intercourse with a new partner, *tell him about your fears straight out* (he may have similar fears). Say, "I like you and I want sex with you but I'm very worried about disease. I'm not implying that you're ill and that I don't trust you, but help my peace of mind. Please tell me if you have anything now or have had in the past, and if you've had lots of partners recently. If you're not sure, let's use a condom or put off intercourse for now."

It's not easy to speak out openly, especially if you're both "hot," candles flickering, wine glowing in goblets, but *romance is one thing and venereal disease is another*. Be realistic, it's your body! Being outspoken can help avoid worry and illness.

Think about this if you hesitate to ask such questions: If he's about to kiss you, and he's been coughing and sneezing, you'd probably say, "If you have a cold, let's put off the kissing until next time." Why not talk as plainly about V.D.?

Also, if you're very active sexually, you might carry some condoms for self-protection. There's no guarantee that the precautions here will work—your best protection is being extra careful, frank, and knowing that the more promiscuous you are, the greater the possibility of catching a sexually transmitted disease.

Fear of homosexuality (man): "I attended a company convention and was assigned a roommate. After going to sleep drunk, I was awakened by his climbing into my bed. In a daze I felt him sucking me off—enjoyed it, and let go. I have a wonderful wife, kids, a good sex life, now I fear I may be a homosexual. How can I restore my peace of mind and enjoy sex fully with my wife again?"

What you had is called a "situational" homosexual experience, initiated by your roommate. You were both intoxicated. Instead of rejecting the man, you allowed yourself to go along. All right, it happened. But an isolated episode doesn't turn you into a homosexual. Nor does it mean that you were a homosexual all along. Having been heterosexual all your life and enjoying a good sex life with your wife, there's no need to worry that you've changed overnight.

Many people have situational homosexual experiences . . . when deprived of women while in the service, or in other circumstances without women. Also many heterosexual adolescents have experienced some homosexual experimentation. Unless you continue to fantasize about men and homosexual intercourse since that one occasion, my advice is to erase it from your memory. In a similar situation, watch your alcohol consumption. Make sure that whatever you do, you have a clear head and full awareness of the consequences.

Virginity (woman): "I'm twenty-three, still a virgin for two main reasons: First, my standard is to love a man deeply in order to have intercourse with him. I've never been really in love before. Second, now I love a man who loves me and wants us to marry eventually. I'd like to go all the way with him but fear of pain and bleeding the first time, and perhaps other complications, are blocking me. How can I overcome my fears?''

Good reasoning, there's nothing wrong with being a virgin! Relax—no need to fear pain, bleeding, other complications. Sex is a normal function, with the body designed for relatively easy sex.

Basically, this is what happens normally during first intercourse: The man inserts his erect penis into the vagina, widens the opening of the hymen, which just retracts. Most women scarcely feel any pain. Bleeding ranges from zero to some staining as if having a period. Women who report much pain and excessive bleeding usually have an inept, inexperienced, even brutal partner. Or the woman is very tense, ignorant, with distorted views about female anatomy and what happens during intercourse.

Now that your knowledge has been expanded, I suggest that you go into the E.F. float, and imagine actual delightful sexual intercourse with the man you love. Think of giving, receiving, of mutual great enjoyment. Tell him that you're a virgin and need gentle, loving care.

Breast inadequacy (woman): ''My breasts are very small, and that fact has always interfered with my fullest enjoyment of sex. My husband says he loves me, not just my breasts, but I've heard him tell friends humorously that he goes for 'big boobs.' I've considered having breast augmentation surgery but

am a physical coward. How can I get over this sex-ual hangup?''

Realize clearly that there is much more to being a woman than having big breasts. If you still feel self-conscious about small breasts, here are some effective paths to a solution:

Start by doing some soul-searching—ask yourself *why* it is so important to you to have big breasts, espe-cially if your husband seems satisfied, and your rela-tionship is good? In my clinical experience, I've often found that women who feel that their breasts are too small have problems in terms of their body-image, and *a general feeling of insecurity as a woman, or as a person.*

If the latter is true, then whatever the size of your breasts, you wouldn't be satisfied. Consider the case of one of my patients, Alice—twenty-six, attractive, di-vorced. She was referred to me by a plastic surgeon who had strong doubts about performing breast aug-mentation on her. She'd had *three* previous breast oper-ations, two augmentations, and a reduction because she then considered her breasts to be oversize.

After talking with Alice, it became obvious that no surgical breast procedure would ever satisfy her—because she was a very insecure, confused and unhappy human being. I told her that, and recommended psy-chotherapy first to help her develop her personality. Then her request for further breast surgery could be re-evaluated.

In your instance, if your self-esteem is high, consider trying to overcome your obsession about the size of your breasts by learning to *like* rather than hate them. Consider too that small breasts are usually more attractive than large, hanging breasts in the aging process. It's a matter of personal taste.

Here's a suggestion that has worked for many in learning how to like your breasts, whatever size they are: Go into the E.F. float, and picture yourself nude on your inner TV screen. Examine and critically evaluate all parts of your body, from top to toe. Note what you consider are your strong and weak points.

Now, having taken a survey of yourself, start to accentuate your strong points and minimize your weak ones. If you have long, slender legs—a great turn-on for most men—show them off with especially attractive shoes, stockings, skirts. If you have beautiful teeth, reveal them with an appealing smile and lovely lipstick. In short, *accentuate your positives*.

Next, erect posture can improve the appearance of breasts measurably. Start sitting up, standing, walking straight. You'll be delighted with the improvement in how your bosom looks. If you stoop over to hide your small breasts, you pull negative attention to that area. Imagine that your breasts are large, and carry them proudly—you'll probably look at least one size bigger.

After all that, if you're still convinced that your breasts are inadequate, you may think in depth about plastic surgery. Seek a plastic surgeon recommended by your family physician, by friends who have had similar successful procedures, or call your local medical society for reputable names. Don't settle for "cheap." Plastic surgery is a serious procedure, not a "beauty shop treatment."

Suspicion of cheating (woman): "**My live-in partner of three years doesn't seem as interested in sex the** past few months. I think he's playing around, so I turn away when he reaches for me. It's spoiling our relationship. What can I do?''

Your turning away from your man at night is a statement of your anger at him. Here's my suggestion:

First, in the relaxation and focused concentration of your E.F. float, ask yourself if your suspicion comes from *insecurity within yourself*—which you choose to interpret as his lack of interest, resulting in his turning to another woman. But, diminished sexual interest can also be due to other factors such as stress, depression, fatigue. If you can rule out these possibilities, and are certain that there is another woman, confront the issue with him, although it's difficult and painful. Obviously, you can't force him to be monogamous, but you should have a choice—to accept or reject him.

Think it through. What made him get involved with someone else? Have there been problems and dissatisfactions in your relationship that you denied? Was it really not going well, yet you didn't want to face it? Reevaluate the situation, then work out the problems, or dissolve the relationship.

Performance Anxiety

Lack of confidence inhibits sex life (woman): "I'm forty, considered attractive, but my sexual experience has been limited because of working all hours to support my invalided parents. Now I've reached executive status, but I avoid men since I lack confi-

dence to satisfy them sexually. How can I change my scared attitude?''

The fact that your sexual experience is limited is no reason for you to avoid sex. You worry that you won't satisfy a man sexually. Focus instead on the fact that sex is not a performance but *a way of communicating love and affection.* If you meet a man, and there is mutual liking and regard, tell him openly that you feel anxious because you haven't had much experience.

Most men won't see this as negative, but will probably be more gentle and considerate. It's even flattering for a man to know that you've been very selective and not gotten involved with ''anybody'' who came along. *Avoidance won't solve your problem or increase your self-confidence,* so communicate.

Correcting failure at intercourse (man): **''I'm in shock, hope you can help. I've been okay with sex until now. I met this beautiful woman in my office. I'm kind of homely and short, so I was surprised when she accepted a date. On our third date, we went to bed. I was so excited that when we kissed, I came immediately, not even in her yet. I couldn't get an erection again and left in shame. How can I correct my failure and be a man with her?''**

You experienced an episode of *premature ejaculation.* It happens, especially to young men who haven't learned ejaculatory control. It also can occur at almost any age due to intense excitement and performance anxiety. (Women too sometimes have premature orgasm but that's usually considered a sign of ''passion,'' not a problem.)

Premature ejaculation is readily treatable, especially

if it happens only occasionally, as with you. Ask her for another date, and don't avoid sexual contact. Then do this:

1. *Go into E.F. several times daily* and fantasize about her. Imagine all kinds of sexual situations together. As you familiarize yourself with her this way, it becomes less sexually frightening when you're with her.

2. *Right before sex with her, go into E.F.*, the quick way, so you'll be fully relaxed physically, and focused mentally. Bring her to orgasm at least *once* before you insert your penis. Having her climax will relieve your "performance anxiety." In 25 to 30 percent of men with premature ejaculation, this alone is the cure.

After you've helped her come once or more through masturbation, oral pleasuring, or using a vibrator, and you're ready to insert your penis, focus only on the *pleasure you feel in your genitals*. Don't be so concerned with her now—she's had her orgasms, and it's your turn. Sex should be enjoyment by both partners.

3. If these steps don't alleviate your problem, try the following program which has helped many others. Now you'll have to tell your partner that you have trouble controlling your excitement, and need her help. If she loves or likes you enough, she'll agree gladly. Proceed this way:

Stage 1: Lie on your back, then go into E.F. and enjoy the relaxed, clearminded feeling. You are ready to "receive," not to "perform." You are about to raise the threshold of your excitement, so you won't ejaculate prematurely. Your partner should stroke you manually or orally until you are close to coming, but right before you ejaculate, she should stop and *squeeze* *your penis,* right behind the head, for 15 to 20 seconds—then release.

At this point, your erection is halfway down, and there's no urge to ejaculate. After 30 seconds, do it all over again. When you're about to climax, she stops, squeezes, and your penis goes partially limp. This is the *squeeze technique,* used successfully by many sex therapists. Repeat the squeeze technique several times daily or nightly for one to two days.

Stage 2: Now that you're both experts in the squeeze technique, add this. After the squeeze process, with your penis half limp, she should sit on you and "stuff" the semi-flaccid penis into her vagina. Now, she slides slowly up and down on your penis. You are in E.F., enjoying the sensation without activity on your part.

Right before you come, say "Stop!"—until the urge subsides. Start again, stop again. Repeat a few times daily. In a week or two, you'll have gained full control of your orgasms, and learned when to slow up, to make your erection last to give and receive maximum satisfaction.

Wife/mistress potency problem (man): **"I'm in great physical shape, successful, happily married, two kids, but with a real sexual problem. I've become involved with my secretary, enjoying my best sex ever. Now I just can't get it up with my wife, though I'm terrific with my mistress. My wife is worried too, and it could be tragic if she suspects I'm playing around. How can I be potent with her?"**

Guilt is a prime antiaphrodisiac. You probably feel guilty about "cheating" on your wife. Accordingly, *your penis is symbolically frightened to erect because of fear of punishment!* The unconscious is a very potent opera-tor! Before you can restore potency with your wife, you must do some honest soul-searching. Ask yourself, "Why did I get involved with my secretary in the first place? Is it an overwhelming physical attraction . . . or dissatisfaction in my marriage?"

To find the true answer, I suggest you use the E.F. screen technique for clear insights. Ask, "Does some-thing specific in my relationship with my wife upset me so much that I became involved with another to coun-teract my dissatisfaction?"

In a parallel situation, a patient, Gary, suddenly re-alized through an E.F. replay that he was angry with his wife, Netta, for giving all her attention to their new-born infant. He felt neglected and rejected. "So," he told me, as a revelation, "wanting love desperately, I fell for a young secretary who'd been in my company for two years. She gave me the affection I craved."

At my suggestion, Netta joined us in therapy. When he explained, she said in shock, "I thought Gary was acting odd, coming home late, but I was so preoccupied with the baby, I didn't say anything." With clarifica-tion and understanding, he ended his affair and re-turned to his wife. His erections returned too.

Answering the question directly: Applying the E.F. concentration exercise repeatedly can help you find the right answer. Realize that your wife, children, secre-tary, all will be affected by your decision, *so be fully aware of the consequences*. If your solution is still unclear, consider professional counseling. Once you choose and act, your erection problem should be alleviated.

Physical and Medical Problems

Fear of heart attack (woman): "Since my husband's shocking heart attack six months ago (he's only thirty-eight), the doctor has said he's recovered enough for us to enjoy intercourse again. We've tried, but my husband stops, mumbles, 'I can't risk another attack—you'd better find somebody else for sex.' I don't want anybody else, I love him. Help, please, or our marriage will collapse. How can I restore his self-confidence?"

Don't despair. Patients who've had close calls, as in recovering from heart attack (M.I., myocardial infarction), may fear any effort, including sexual activity. They may experience severe depression and anxiety may grow, possibly leading to erection problems in a man. There is hope, as in this comparable case:

A couple—Ned, forty-one, and Marie, thirty-eight—visited me six months after his heart attack. "We're both on our second marriage," she explained. "My first husband died of a cerebral hemorrhage during sexual intercourse. I've had therapy to overcome my burden of loss and guilt. Now we've been happily married for seven years, enjoyed great sex . . . until Ned's attack."

Ned took over, "After my doctor's okay, I wanted sex again. But we failed because Marie is so uptight. Neither of us spoke up. Her repressed fears added to my deep terror. I began to doubt my masculinity, and worried about losing my potency forever."

"Our bedroom became a battlefield of unbearable tensions," Marie interjected. "Finally we're here . . . can you help us?"

"I think I can help you help yourselves." Here's the basic treatment approach that worked for them, and for others.

Step 1: I insisted that Ned have a thorough checkup again, so we'd all know the medical facts about his current condition, effects of his medication, his physician's recommendations on physical activities and lifestyle—smoking, diet, work, sex.

Step 2: They both learned E.F. for thorough relaxation. They were to go into E.F. at bedtime to undo the negative tensions associated with the bedroom. They said it worked.

Step 3: A week later I taught them the procedure for *overcoming impotence* (Chapter 11) . . . and positions to use in intercourse to reduce exertion and lessen the likelihood of heart strain. The common "missionary" position (man on top) was to be avoided since it requires sustained arm and shoulder muscle contraction. Preferred positions are side-by-side or female on top, less physically stressful for the man.

Step 4: I recommended that both abstain from smoking and alcohol, heavy evening meals, arguments, pressure conflicts.

Step 5: I encouraged Ned to join a cardiac program approved by his doctor, with exercises designed to increase blood flow to the cardiac arteries, thus boosting his physical and sexual fitness. I impressed on *both* that sexual intercourse is generally no more strenuous than climbing two flights of stairs (a measure some doctors use to check ability to resume sexual activity).

Step 6: Very important, we spoke openly about the issue of life and death, which they had avoided. Talking about it removed much underlying fear and anxiety. They agreed to exchange feelings candidly in the future.

Result: They resumed their normal sex life within a few weeks, and reported that they enjoyed greater intimacy and love than during the previous seven years of marriage!

To you I suggest a similar strategy—after full discussion and agreement with your doctor. In some very severe cases, involving certain specific complications, sexual alternatives requiring less muscular exertion may be recommended, such as mutual masturbation and/or oral sex.

Overweight to avoid sex? (woman): **"I'm extremely overweight, obese—have been for years. Now thirty, my sex life is nil. I've heard that some women, and men too, stay purposely fat without realizing it—to avoid sex. I've failed at reducing, I love food too much. I'm now starved for sex—I want a man bad. Any hope for me?"**

It is understandable that you're starved for sex because, by thirty, most women have established a regular sex life. Being overweight doesn't necessarily mean that you can't find a man who's attracted to you. Yes, some overweight women avoid social situations where they'd meet men. This usually intensifies the dilemma because the less you mix and socialize, the more upset and hopeless you feel. As a result, you eat even more! The problem is usually twofold: Your being overweight and your difficulties relating to men and sex.

Work on the solutions simultaneously. If you wait until you've taken off a lot of weight, you'll lose valuable time. Start *now* to date and relate to a man. And, being obese, it's urgent to join a medically accepted weight reduction program. Use E.F. also to help focus your mind on your goal of sustained weight loss.

As you begin socializing, be aware of men who show interest in you. If you're invited on a date, *don't avoid it because of your weight* (you're fixing that). Once involved with a man, your desire for food is likely to decrease since you won't be substituting food for love.

Wife's body kills sex urge (man): **"I love my wife's mind and character, but her body repels me now. She weighs forty pounds more than when we married ten years ago. I resist sex, and she doesn't seem to mind. Other slimmer women attract me, and I'm afraid I'll start having affairs and ruin our marriage. What can I do to have satisfying sex with her again?"**

Before having an affair, discuss quietly and frankly with your wife how you feel about her weight gain—but analyze your marriage first. If there's considerable weight gain by a spouse, it may indicate marital dissatisfaction. When two people are close day after day, they must work at being loving and caring despite pressures, changes in lifestyle, conflicts.

Women are especially likely to overeat because of tension and frustration. Particularly women who give up careers to become homemakers may start nibbling in the kitchen, spurred by feelings of resentment, anger, boredom.

It's vital to bring everything out in the open. Then

both of you discuss the right approach to lose weight. If this doesn't help restore her desired weight, and friction continues, you might see a qualified therapist together. Find out if there's a more serious underlying problem, medically or emotionally.

Post-prostate sex denial (woman): "Since my husband's prostate surgery, he refuses to have sex, even though the doctor says he's perfectly capable. But my man insists that he can't perform, that he's finished with sex. How can I convince him otherwise?"

Please have your husband study these *facts* carefully: Ten percent of all men by age forty, and fifty percent by age eighty, have an enlarged prostate, mostly related to changes in hormone levels. Therefore large numbers of men have prostate surgery. Unfortunately and unnecessarily for the vast majority, some men experience temporary impotence after the surgery, *primarily psychologically induced.*

A dominant reason for such transient avoidance of sex is the misconception that the prostate trouble was caused by intercourse, and further sex could make the problem worsen. Furthermore, some men feel that surgery on any part of the genital apparatus is a form of *castration,* with ensuing impotence. *Anatomically this is not true.* The prostate has nothing to do with the mechanism of erection. It is involved specifically in adding volume to the ejaculate (the fluids that come together with semen when having an orgasm).

Nevertheless, some men think after a prostate operation that they can't "get it up" anymore. Such firm belief tends to fulfill their own prophecy. As stated earlier, the brain is most important in the cycle of sexual arousal, and if the brain turns off on this, the penis will not turn on!

You, as the wife, must be gentle and understanding—*don't push him*. Point out the fact that recurrent, normal nocturnal and early-morning erections prove that his impotence is psychological, not physical. Tell him you'll wait for intercourse until he's ready again; meanwhile both can enjoy the sustaining intimacy of kissing, hugging, caressing, fondling.

Suggest too that he relax in the Erotic Focus float up to ten times daily, that he get the pleasure of fantasizing in E.F. He can renew his sexuality further by following instructions for overcoming impotence (Chapter 11), and doing the sexual exercises for men. These steps uaually lead to sexual renewal.

Hysterectomy ruining sex life (man): "I'm desperate! We're both in our midthirties, but since my wife's hysterectomy several months ago, she says she's lot her sexiness and feminine attractiveness. She won't permit intercourse, won't believe she's just as sexy to me. How can I get her back to where we were before her hysterectomy?"

Mutual understanding is the key. A hysterectomy is psychologically traumatic for some women (not all), who exaggerate the functional importance of the uterus in relation to femininity and sexual attractiveness. Actually the uterus, no larger than a small fist in the non-pregnant state, *has no role in the mechanism of sexual arousal and orgasm. The uterus gives no pleasurable or other sensations during sexual intercourse.* It's just the organ in which the fetus develops.

Try this: Have your wife read the preceding organic facts. Then reassure her of your continued loving feelings. Suggest that she use the Erotic Focus method to help eliminate her tensions and misconceptions. She should project on her "inner screen" exactly what is upsetting her about having had her uterus removed.

For instance, is it the idea that she cannot have children? Is it fear that her hormones will not be the same? Is it concern that there may be physical changes reducing her sexual enjoyment? She should see her gynecologist for a detailed explanation of exactly what was done, what physical changes might be expected, if any, and effects on her sexual functioning.

In E.F., your wife should try to identify any psychological conflicts about her sense of feminine identification, such as: "Now that I've lost female organs, am I less of a woman? Will my husband seek out someone else?" "If he wants children, will he divorce me?"

Encourage your wife to discuss any such conflicts openly with you. If she can't speak up, and continues to be upset, psychotherapy may be needed to help her adjust. (I do suggest that every woman undergoing surgical removal of her uterus, ovaries or breasts should have a consultation with a psychiatrist/psychologist. Or if the surgeon is psychologically aware, he should talk at length with the patient beforehand.)

Sexual fears before period—PMS (woman): "I'm thirty-five, married. My husband and I have good sex, except eight to ten days before my period. During that time, I lose sexual desire, I feel miserable—

depressed, irritable, angry. My gynecologist says I have PMS (Premenstrual Syndrome). He wants to put me on hormones, but I'm fearful. Is there anything else I can do?"

PMS differs in each woman suffering from it (usually more prevalent with advancing years). It's now recognized generally as an incapacitating affliction, related to hormone problems before the menstrual cycle. Mood, behavior and sexual responses are involved with differing hormonal levels which may change each month.

PMS symptoms may begin from two weeks to a day before menstruation—with at least a week of *no* symptoms after the period. This cessation helps differentiate PMS depression from an ongoing depression. If you think you have PMS (by no means occurring to all women), thorough examination by your internist or gynecologist is essential. Treatment usually includes the patient keeping a diary of physical and psychological symptoms, among other measures.

Physical symptoms (which don't necessarily mean you have PMS) may include: Feeling bloated (due to water retention), swelling of the feet, hands, weight gain with increased appetite and specific cravings (especially sweets), breast pain/tenderness, hot flushes, headaches, pelvic discomfort (abdominal cramps), changes in bowel habits or increased thirst.

Psychological symptoms may include: Depression, heightened aggression, irritability, tension, anxiety, fatigue, sleep problems, decrease or increase in sexual desire, lowered concentration ability, imparied judgment (obviously, such generalized symptoms don't *necessarily* indicate PMS).

Treatment approaches vary greatly, and are controversial at this time. The range covers use of hormones, oral contraceptives, diuretics, certain vitamins, a variety of medications. Most doctors include dietary restrictions (especially coffee, alcohol, sugar, salt), rest, exercise, avoiding high stress situations.

The Erotic Focus technique has helped many of my patients as part of "what-to-do" as soon as the slightest PMS symptoms appear. Go into the E.F. float, using pleasant imagery to soothe and distract yourself. For instance, if your symptoms include pelvic congestion and cramps, then focus on relaxing muscles in that area (such tension release promotes better blood circulation). As you visualize the inside of your pelvic area during E.F., go on a "body trip" (see Chapter 10). Visualize the internal pelvic area rather than the vagina (perhaps a glance at a basic anatomy book will help).

Since PMS affects the sexual life of many women, and E.F. can be a specific aid, I must emphasize again that it is imperative to be checked by a gynecologist. The findings lead to *knowledge* and remedial treatment, relieving what may be baseless fears.

Sex During Pregnancy and After

Fear of partner getting pregnant (man): "A friend living with a woman for two years trusted her to take contraceptive measures. Then she said she'd gone off the pill without telling him, was pregnant, wanted a baby with or without marriage. I dread the same happening to me since my partner says she can't come if I use a condom. I find myself with-drawing before orgasm. Neither of us gets full satis-faction, and my fear makes me wilt. Help, please.''

It's unfair when a woman goes off the pill without telling her partner. The decision to have a child should always be a mutual one. Yes, a woman may decide to have a child and bring it up on her own, but the man should be informed of the intent—then he can decide whether or not he wants to father the child or not. If his answer is negative, the woman should respect that. She can get impregnated elsewhere, or apply to a sperm bank.

In your case, my advice is to have a serious talk with your girlfriend. Establish a solid understanding about mutual feelings about pregnancy and how to deal with that if it should occur. Discuss abortion too. Open, honest communication is a *must*. If you can't trust and respect each other, reexamine your relationship.

In terms of contraception, perhaps visit her gynecol-ogist together for advice on the safest and most effective method for your needs. Then, put your worries aside, use E.F. to block out intruding concerns, and enjoy sex thoroughly.

Sex during pregnancy (woman): ''My obstetrician said intercourse up to the last weeks of pregnancy wouldn't harm the fetus—but we're not enjoying sex much. I can't let go because I feel it might harm the baby. At times when I'm near orgasm, my hus-band asks, 'Am I hurting you?'—and I poop out. Can you help?''

It will help you both to understand that at different

stages of pregnancy, guidelines for sexual intercourse change:

1. *First trimester:* There's no reason why early pregnancy should restrict sexual activity—unless there is bleeding or other physical problems occur to be checked with your obstetrician. You may get some morning sickness which inhibits sex in the morning. If excessive fatigue develops during the day, it may dissipate desire for sex at night. Otherwise, for most couples, this is a period of special mutual sexual enjoyment and closeness. Consider sex in the afternoon or very early evening, before energy drops.

Some women experience a loss of sexual interest particularly in a first trimester. In addition to problems mentioned, there may be physiological changes such as painful breast engorgement, sometimes accentuated by sexual arousal. But *don't anticipate any negatives;* many couples enjoy an upsurge in sexual pleasures.

Be reassured—there is no conclusive evidence that intercourse during the first trimester can cause spontaneous abortion of the fetus. Yes, some women are anxious, especially if they've had miscarriages. Miscarriages and spontaneous abortions are most likely to occur during this period, if at all, caused by a variety of factors. Only 10 to 15 percent are due to sexual intercourse.

2. *Second trimester:* Be heartened that most women report *surging interest and sexual satisfaction.* Some women find sex better than at any other time, including when they are not pregnant! That's because any nausea, vomiting, and extreme fatigue have passed, and there's no breast soreness during intercourse. Vaginal lubrica-

tion may be considerably increased, especially in women who have given birth before.

Practically all coital positions can generally be used now (no spectacular acrobatics, of course). And of course there's no fear of becoming pregnant. If, near the end of this period, some positions become tiring or uncomfortable, you'll adjust accordingly.

3. *Third trimester:* There's no clear medical evidence that sex even now is "bad" or unhealthy for the baby, or may induce premature labor. Very late in this period, some women feel contractions of the uterine muscles during orgasm, but these usually don't induce labor. The uterus may go into spasm up to one minute following orgasm, resulting in an "odd" but not painful sensation (some women find it especially thrilling).

Most couples reduce sexual activity for various reasons. Some obstetricians advise patients to either abstain completely during these last months, or for the final four to six weeks. This is primarily to avoid the possibility of infecting the fetus. Physically, some women feel uncomfortable, perhaps with backaches, increased urinary frequency, fatigue. On the positive side, intimacy is enhanced, as the last few weeks are filled with joyous anticipation.

With increased understanding and reassurance now, I hope your anxieties are alleviated. Furthermore, you'll get wonderful help by learning and using the Erotic Focus method, a great aid too during labor to attain maximum relaxation with natural childbirth, the LaMaze technique, or other delivery procedure.

Go into the E.F. float for extra ease and enjoyment of intercourse. And, again, *communicate*. If you are at all uncomfortable, speak up, share—don't wait for him to ask. Agree beforehand that you'll tell him how to move, to stop if necessary. Thus, uncertainties you mention are avoided, no need to be concerned when sexually excited.

Late in the second trimester, and in the third, the most comfortable sexual position for many is side by side. Also you on top, lying face down on him, or straddling him and sitting up—that means less pressure. And remember the "doggy" position, you on hands and knees, your husband entering your vagina from the rear (your pregnant belly rests on the bed, no downward compression), affording the man easy entrance.

It's fun to be creative together; it's a new sexual adventure! He can sit on a comfortable chair, you straddling his lap, facing or your back to him. Your pregnant tummy isn't in the way—you're both free to move and touch wherever you like.

In the final four to six weeks, you may prefer to abstain from intercourse, but *don't miss out on the special togetherness*. Use E.F. even more often, both enjoying intimate, sexual fantasies and enhanced anticipation. Pleasure each other with gentle caressing, some mutual masturbation, perhaps (but no probing with fingers in the vagina, a possible source of infection at this time). With oral sex, you can bring him to orgasm, but it's better for you that his tongue not enter your vagina.

Just being close, nestling, fondling, caressing brings extraordinary joy right up to the moment of birth.

Sex after baby's birth (man): "It's two months since our baby was born, but my wife still won't let me near her in bed. She says she's exhausted taking care of the infant. Preoccupied with new motherhood, she isn't interested in sex, or in me. I don't want to look for sex outside, but I'm frustrated. What can I do?"

You have a tough problem that can be handled with *understanding* leading to solution. Basically, realize that patterns in sexual activity after delivery vary greatly. Six weeks is considered the norm, but it may be earlier or later, depending on the couple. There's possibility of infection until everything is healed and back to normal, subject to the doctor's okay. Some women feel physical discomfort when returning to sex at first, and this is related to complete healing. Check with your doctor to make sure that everything has completely healed physically. Here's an example: A patient consulted me because of intense pain during intercourse after her second baby. Her gynecologist brushed it off as "emotional" and "avoidance behavior." I took a very careful sexual history which revealed that she didn't want to avoid sex. Quite the opposite—she was aroused and eager, but every time she and her husband tried intercourse, she was in pain. She was fine with mutual masturbation but not penis insertion.

A checkup by another gynecologist revealed she'd had a tight, faulty episiotomy (incision at the vaginal entrance). The specialist made the repair, which healed perfectly, and she resumed enjoyable normal sexual relations.

Here's my advice: You say your wife is too "exhausted" for sexual intercourse. How about pitching in to take care of the baby, provide some relief? You'll find it personally rewarding, too.

Instead of the usual nighttime approach, try making love in the morning after the baby is fed, or afternoon or early evening before her weariness sets in. If she breast feeds, a good time is right after feeding. The baby is quiet and probably sleeping and your wife, like many women, is probably partially aroused by the baby sucking her nipples.

This should help, but if she still focuses totally on her infant, discuss quietly and seriously why she is an over-anxious mother. Point out that you love the baby too, but you love her as a person more than ever, and she's not being fair to you in denying you her attention and affection. It's not infrequent for a first-time mother to lose her perspective, and need reawakening. Once realization comes, the marriage is usually much stronger and even more loving and sexually fulfilling.

14

Getting Professional Sex Therapy, If Needed

You now know that by practice and use of the Erotic Focus method, you have an innovative and *proved successful* approach to enjoying better sex for the rest of your life. In addition, the many suggestions and recommendations will add to your multiple rewards and fulfillment due to much improved sexual activity. Feel assured that the material you have at hand is not empty theory or vague assumption. Beneficial results for people of practically all adult ages have been demonstrated from the advice in this book.

However, the Erotic Focus method is not the one sure and unfailing way to attain better sex, nor is it the single and total solution for all sexual problems. But I can and do affirm that my techniques, as provided for you in this book, have worked for thousands of others.

But in cases where more serious psychological complications exist, highly skilled and more intensive therapy may well be indicated. As with all qualified psychiatrists, psychologists, and thoroughly trained, authorized and licensed sex therapists (not just self-labeled "sex therapists"), extended treatment may be necessary. Here is just one example from my experience . . .

Thawing Sexual Freeze-Up

A twenty-one-year-old college student, Pam, was referred to me by her gynecologist as burdened with severe psychological problems. When she visited the specialist, she had almost hysterically demanded a *hymenectomy* (surgical removal of her hymen, the fold of membrane usually partially closing the orifice of the vagina in a virgin). The doctor had finally persuaded her to confer with me before any further action could be considered.

I found Pam attractive, her eyes bright and alert but very frightened, even frantic. Her history emerged over weeks of essential deeper therapy. She revealed her exceptional panic about sexual activity. This terror had been increasing since she had reached puberty at age twelve.

She had dated quite often in her teen years, but always held the boys at arm's length. For three months at college, she had seen just one boyfriend, Ted. They engaged in kissing and petting, but no sexual intercourse. When he finally pushed her hard to yield, she froze up, told him she was a virgin, and was "scared to death."

He reacted angrily, "I don't want to mess with that!" He stopped seeing her.

Anguished, she told me, "I was heartbroken. I know

he left me because of my being a virgin, with no sexual experience, and always jumpy and afraid. I dated two more men, and I tried to have intercourse. But I always would freeze up again . . . and I've finally just about given up . . ."

She blurted out, "I must have my hymen removed surgically, that's my only chance to have normal sex. I'm sure that will wipe out my dread of the blood and pain, because I'll no longer be a virgin. Then I can act human. I get hot, I want sex, *but I can't let go!*"

Steps in Therapy (Remedial Treatment)

First, Erotic Focus relief: Pam responded well when I said that, to start, I'd teach her a simple exercise to help her relax and be clearheaded whenever a situation leading to intercourse arose in the future. During her visits, we included reinforcement practice in the E.F. technique. She said she felt a greater sense of peace of mind and relaxation almost immediately. She was still somewhat tense and anxious about sex, but less so. She stopped pressing for hymen removal surgery.

Simultaneously, we progressed with her therapy.

After she emerged, calmed, from her relaxing and refreshing state of E.F., we discussed her feelings about sexuality. Together we examined her moral standards. It became quite clear that she was a relatively shy and insecure person, which, I pointed out, was not unusual for her age. It developed as she spoke that, "I disapprove strongly of the sexual promiscuity I see on campus. Yet . . . I'm at a big disadvantage socially because of morals and virginity." She agonized, "I'm not part of the scene because I won't go all the way sexually." Her decision to have the hymenectomy was based on not feeling accepted in the campus life she craved.

I stated that in some cases there are medical reasons to have a hymenectomy. But I underscored that her gynecological examinations and tests had established conclusively that such surgery was definitely not indicated or advisable in her instance. I explained that to proceed with surgery, just for the purpose of deception about her virginity, would add up to a statement of severe insecurity. Just removing the hymen would not make her more experienced sexually, and thus would not relieve basic anxieties about intercourse. Hiding the facts about one's virginity—as though this were something to be ashamed of (which it certainly is not), would be an unfortunate and forebodingly mixed up beginning to a person's sex life.

When sex occurs in an atmosphere of mutual caring and trust, the first intercourse experience can be most meaningful and pleasurable to both partners, I emphasized. This affirmative joining develops after establishing an open channel of honest communication on sexual matters, not from make-believe.

Pam was not unique in that every woman, and man too, starts out *as a beginner* sexually. I emphasized that a man who is not willing to put up with the special "effort" of understanding the fear and anxiety of a woman's initial such experience, is not likely to be a desirable partner at any time.

Next Stage in the Therapeutic Process

After several weeks of this person-to-person therapy, I suggested a hiatus in our sessions. I advised Pam to continue with her E.F. exercises up to ten times daily, as convenient, then to return when she felt the urge or need.

She came back six weeks later. She had met another man, "I'm in love with him—I think for the first time for real." She said that they had kissed and petted, now both felt ready to go "all the way." She wanted a reinforcement session in talk and E.F. because, "I feel like a new woman, but—I'll admit—I'm still a bit tense and anxious about my virginity. I can't take any chances about losing Larry."

As the next step, I taught her the "Stage-by-Stage Treatment" in Chapter 10, as detailed there to correct and overcome anorgasmia. She agreed eagerly, certain that Larry would cooperate fully and enthusiastically, after I stressed that his participation was essential for the most remedial result.

Promising outcome: Pam phoned the next day, sounding wonderfully exhilarated . . . "I apologize. I'm afraid that we didn't follow your program exactly in detail. I told all the steps to Larry, and we started working on the treatment right away. Well, we both went into E.F.—I'd taught him soon after we met. The next steps just followed naturally. We were both so sexually aroused that we simply couldn't stop. It happened, he was in me—*oh!*" She broke off, giggling.

I waited. She went on, "Amazingly, there was no pain. A little discomfort . . . a pressure sensation . . . but . . . it was wonderful. We had sex several times through the night and we both were wild about it. And we love each other so much more . . . it's like a miracle . . .''

No miracle. Just needed therapy. And this time it was apparently thoroughly effective.

Choosing a Therapist

I urge you to always give your Erotic Focus Self-Treatment Program time to help you. Enough practice may well be all you need before the technique works for you fully, as proved with so many others. If, after a period of weeks, you still haven't gotten over your pressing difficulty, you might consider seeking the help of a qualified, professional therapist. Here are suggested steps you can take:

1. *First have a thorough physical examination* to rule out conclusively the absence of any organic causes for your sexual problems.

2. *Ask your doctor* to recommend a qualified, medically trained, experienced psychiatrist, psychologist, or a qualified therapist (preferably a physician) with a solid success record in treating sexual problems.

3. *Ask at the nearest medical center,* hospital, or other reputable medical facility for recommendations to find the right, professionally certified therapist for sexual problems.

4. *Beware of individuals advertising themselves* and/or making outright claims that they can overcome your problem speedily and without question. Such promises

are overwhelmingly fallacious. Check the person's professional credentials—then doublecheck. Note my previous assertions that for those with severe sexual problems, E.F. in itself is not a therapy, it is *a valuable tool and aid* that can help make a good therapy program work best for you.

5. *Be wary of one-technique practitioners* who know just a limited type of therapy, yet state that it's the only program that will work perfectly for you. Such therapists obviously have an ax to grind in pushing one specific form of therapy as the solution for you, irrespective of your individual needs. Furthermore, understand that just because an individual claims to be a "sex therapist" is not sufficient qualification, as such declarations are generally not well policed, and may be no more than empty assertions or mere words printed on a paper or sign, with no justification or proof.

6. *Before you decide on the professional* with whom you'll start treatment, be certain that you like, respect, and have a feeling of confidence in working with this individual. Don't hesitate to ask about training and background, details of treatment, fees. If you have any antagonistic reaction, any intuitive distaste or uncertainty about the individual, seek someone else until you are fully satisfied and confident in proceeding.

7. *Consider having your partner come along* after you choose a therapist (checking with the therapist, of course), if you have a strong, longstanding marriage or relationship. As I have stressed often, open communication and understanding are important facets of sexual activity and thorough gratification.

8. *Check referral guides* at your local public library, university and other information centers in your area re-

garding available professional sexual therapists. Some primary sources include: *American Medical Association, American Psychiatric Association, American Psychological Association, The American Society of Clinical Hypnosis, Society for Clinical and Experimental Hypnosis, Sex Information and Education Council of the U.S. (SIECUS), The Sexual Medicine Today Magazine* list of Sexual Dysfunction Clinics.

Tune Up Your Sexuality Lifelong With E.F.

Getting the most from sex and the greatest benefits from the Erotic Focus method merit and require your lifelong practice and pursuit. You can derive utmost rewards in every way for yourself and your loved ones. That is true, of course, in every worthwhile and rewarding endeavor.

As an example, think of this: A knowing guitarist doesn't just pick up the fine instrument and start attacking the strings thoughtlessly and frantically. The true artist begins by cradling the guitar gently, strumming the strings lightly, listening to the responses closely, then tuning up slowly and carefully.

Then, assured that all preparations are exactly right, the peak of perfection attained, the guitarist starts strumming the guitar expertly . . . fully immersed . . . making beautiful music . . .

Your E.F. tune-up functions like that too. You take a minute or two in order to get yourself into the most perfect relaxed, receptive and *alive* state, you focus your concentration clearly toward the lovemaking to come and—with your partner—you rise to the peak of sexual ecstasy and fulfilling love.

This kind of caring approach and zest should always be a part of your life. And, with Erotic Focus, will continue to enrich you as long as you *try*.

Better sex and happier living to YOU!

INDEX